Learning Resources Centre

Today's Social Classes

Series Editor: Cara Acred

Volume 291

Class No.	305 3 HCH
Site	QC 193231
Processed by	
Approved by	

WITHDRAWN

Independence Educational Publishers

First published by Independence Educational Publishers

The Studio, High Green

Great Shelford

Cambridge CB22 5EG

England

© Independence 2016

Copyright

This book is sold subject to the condition that it shall not,
by way of trade or otherwise, be lent, resold, hired out or otherwise
circulated in any form of binding or cover other than that in which it
is published without the publisher's prior consent.

Photocopy licence

The material in this book is protected by copyright. However, the
purchaser is free to make multiple copies of particular articles for instructional
purposes for immediate use within the purchasing institution.
Making copies of the entire book is not permitted.

ISBN-13: 9781861687272

Printed in Great Britain
Zenith Print Group

Contents

Introduction

Today's Social Classes is Volume 291 in the **ISSUES** series. The aim of the series is to offer current, diverse information about important issues in our world, from a UK perspective.

ABOUT TODAY'S SOCIAL CLASSES

Do distinctions between social classes still exist? What about social stereotyping? Does your social class affect the kind of education you receive? This book looks at changing social classes in the UK, social mobility and equality. It also considers issues such as the influence of social class on a person's health, whether students from state schools should be given priority access to university places and the 'digital divide' in the UK.

OUR SOURCES

Titles in the **ISSUES** series are designed to function as educational resource books, providing a balanced overview of a specific subject.

The information in our books is comprised of facts, articles and opinions from many different sources, including:

⇨ Newspaper reports and opinion pieces

⇨ Website factsheets

⇨ Magazine and journal articles

⇨ Statistics and surveys

⇨ Government reports

⇨ Literature from special interest groups

A NOTE ON CRITICAL EVALUATION

Because the information reprinted here is from a number of different sources, readers should bear in mind the origin of the text and whether the source is likely to have a particular bias when presenting information (or when conducting their research). It is hoped that, as you read about the many aspects of the issues explored in this book, you will critically evaluate the information presented.

It is important that you decide whether you are being presented with facts or opinions. Does the writer give a biased or unbiased report? If an opinion is being expressed, do you agree with the writer? Is there potential bias to the 'facts' or statistics behind an article?

ASSIGNMENTS

In the back of this book, you will find a selection of assignments designed to help you engage with the articles you have been reading and to explore your own opinions. Some tasks will take longer than others and there is a mixture of design, writing and research-based activities that you can complete alone or in a group.

FURTHER RESEARCH

At the end of each article we have listed its source and a website that you can visit if you would like to conduct your own research. Please remember to critically evaluate any sources that you consult and consider whether the information you are viewing is accurate and unbiased.

Useful weblinks

www.21stcenturychallenges.org

www.bera.ac.uk/blog

www.britsoc.co.uk

www.cam.ac.uk

blogs.channel4.com

www.theconversation.com

www.ethnicity.ac.uk

www.equalitytrust.org.uk

www.fenews.co.uk

www.thegatewayonline.com

www.theguardian.com

www.huffingtonpost.co.uk

www.independent.co.uk

www.leftfootforward.org

www.manchester.ac.uk

www.nursingtimes.net

www.socialmobility.org.uk

www.telegraph.co.uk

www.yougov.co.uk

Survey charts emergence of new class system

The traditional view of a Britain made up of working, middle and upper class people is no longer accurate, according to one of the largest studies of its kind.

The Great British Class Survey of 161,000 people, has charted the emergence of a new class system comprising seven groups in Britain, blurring the conventional boundaries between the 'middle' and 'working' classes.

It was led by BBC LabUK, and leading sociologists Professor Mike Savage from the London School of Economics and Political Science (LSE) and Professor Fiona Devine from the University of Manchester.

Seven new British social class groups

- Elite
- Established Middle Class
- Technical Middle Class
- New Affluent Workers
- Traditional Working Class
- Emergent Service Workers
- Precariat

The results of the web survey are published in this month's issue of the journal *Sociology*.

According to GBCS, only 39 per cent of Britons now fit the stereotypes of middle and working class – those in the Established middle class and the Traditional working class.

Professor Savage said: "Occupation has been the traditional way to define a person's class, but this is actually too simplistic.

"In fact, social class goes far wider than that: economic, social and cultural dimensions all play an important role.

"So economic capital: income, savings, house value; social capital: the number, and status of people we know; and cultural capital: the extent and nature of cultural interests and activities all play a part."

The 'Technical middle class', a small, distinctive new class group that is prosperous but scores low for social and cultural capital is distinguished by its social isolation and cultural apathy.

'Emergent service workers', a new, young, urban group is relatively poor but has high social and cultural capital.

They appear to be the children of the traditional working class, which has been fragmented by de-industrialisation, mass unemployment, immigration and a shift from manufacturing to service-based employment.

And 'New affluent workers' is another young class group, which is socially and culturally active, with middling levels of economic capital.

Professor Devine said: "Many people think that the problem of social and cultural engagement is more marked in poorer class groups, but the GBCS shows that our levels of social and cultural capital don't always mirror our economic success.

"The Technical middle class score low for social and cultural capital but is quite well off, while the Emergent service workers score highly for cultural and social capital but are not very prosperous.

"The Elite and Precariat groups at the extremes of our class system have been missed in conventional approaches to class analysis, which have focussed on the middle and working classes."

Professor Savage added: "The Elite group is shown to have the most privileged backgrounds also is an important demonstration of the accentuation of social advantage at the top of British society.

"But a relatively old and small traditional working class is fading from contemporary importance."

The seven class groups are:

Elite

This is the most privileged group in the UK. They are set apart from the other six classes, especially because of their wealth, and they have the highest levels of all three capitals.

Established middle class

This is the second wealthiest class group and it scores highly on all three capitals. It is the largest and highly gregarious class group and scores second highest for cultural capital.

Technical middle class

This is a small, distinctive new class group that is prosperous but scores low for social and cultural capital. It is distinguished by its social isolation and cultural apathy.

New affluent workers

This young class group is socially and culturally active, with middling levels of economic capital.

Traditional working class

This class scores low on all forms of capital, but is not completely deprived. Its members have a reasonably high house values, which is explained by this group having the oldest average age (66 years).

Emergent service workers

This new, young, urban group is relatively poor but has high social and cultural capital.

Precariat (the precarious proletariat)

This is the poorest, most deprived class and scores low for social and cultural capital.

Notes for editors

The research team who analysed the data included:

⇨ Dr Niall Cunningham, Professor Yaojun Li and Dr Andrew Miles, all from the University of Manchester.

⇨ Brigitte Le Roux, Associate Professor, Paris Descartes University.

⇨ Professor Johs Hjellbrekke, University of Bergen.

⇨ Dr Mark Taylor, University of York.

⇨ Dr Sam Friedman, City University London, UK.

The paper *A New Model of Social Class? Findings from the BBC's Great British Class Survey Experiment*, was presented in a plenary at the British Sociological Association annual conference. It is available published in the journal *Sociology* and is available at www.bbc.co.uk/science/0/21970879.

4 April 2013

⇨ The above information is reprinted with kind permission from the London School of Economics and Political Science and the University of Manchester. Please visit www.lse.ac.uk or www.manchester.ac.uk for further information. Visit http://www.manchester.ac.uk/discover/news/article/?id=9784 to read the press release in full.

© *London School of Economics and Political Science and the University of Manchester 2015*

Social class in 21st-century Britain: where is the divide now?

Watch* Made in Chelsea *and* The Only Way Is Essex *and you'll see the upper and working classes have more in common than ever. Are we moving away from the old class divides?

By Hannah Betts

Sometimes the most banal social manifestations can prove the most culturally revealing. And so it is with the zeitgeist phenomena that are Channel 4's *Made In Chelsea* (MIC) and ITV's *The Only Way Is Essex* (TOWIE). "Constructed reality" as both are, the denizens of each are supposed to represent distinct social extremes. For *MIC* read: posh, old money, globetrotting, endearingly ghastly metropolitans. For *TOWIE*: chavvy, arriviste, package-holiday-loving, endearingly ghastly suburbanites.

Juxtaposed, the programmes should represent the classic toff/prole face-off, or, at the very least, upper-middle versus lower-middle class. And yet both groups share strikingly similar tastes in clothes, hats, bags, sunglasses, manicures, restaurants, flash cars, bling, booze and ostensibly "upmarket" events such as the races, plus a penchant for fancy dress. Their social and sexual mores are pretty much identical, as is their predilection for fitness, thinness, "street" idiolect, tattoos, launching their own T-shirt lines, family, mutual warfare, Barbours and tiresome small dogs. When brought into contact televisually and at parties, they happily pair off. Were it not for their vowel sounds, it would be difficult to tell them apart.

Is this a sign of working-class/upper-class compatibility? Is it the ever onward march of the middle class, greedily subsuming all? Is it, perhaps, an index of a social circus in which traditional markers have vanished, leaving only the televised and untelevised, moneyed and unmoneyed? Who qualifies as posh and who prole in a world in which big blow-dries, fake tans and tombstone teeth are ubiquitous?

Is Binky Felstead's coffee-coloured, highlighted, champagne-swigging mother any more "classy" than Jessica Wright's, an Essex resident whom you could describe in exactly the same terms? Has "classy" behaviour become detached from class? Is it acceptable to ask all this? In the year 2014 has the byzantine British class system become simpler or more complicated? It is at this point that one's head begins to implode.

Personally, I am classic middle-middle class. Probably. The daughter of a doctor/academic and nurse/full-time mother, I grew up in the second city, went to grammar school and then Oxford, where I taught, and I now work for broadsheet newspapers.

However, immediately there are aspects to confuse matters. My parents were not in the least house-proud, but would spend any money on books. The first play I saw was *Hamlet* at eight. Censorship-wise, we were allowed to read and view anything we wanted, provided we carried it through to the bitter end. Sexual mores were not invigilated. Money was always found for matters cultural, but I did not venture abroad until I was 20, holidays being Scotland or the South Coast. Table manners were not rated as highly as the quality of dinnertime debates, even if we may have said "supper".

All of which once led a social scientist to pronounce my middle-middle protestations a fraud and declare me "upper-middle boho" (what BBC sociologists referred to as "established middle class" in a 2013 class online quiz). That said, my maternal grandfather never spoke to my father on account of the latter having indulged in "book learning", and his own father-in-law possessed no arms, courtesy of an industrial accident. There

are servants not too far back in my lineage, just as there are reckless gambling gentry. At the very least, I have always felt if not socially oblivious then curiously socially relaxed.

When I got in to Oxford, a teacher told me that she hoped I would not end up in a padded cell, driven mad by class angst, like another (state) old girl. Instead, I merely assumed that everyone was like me – which they certainly pretended to be, unlike a fellow grammar-school boy who took up cravats and could be driven mad by the term "hostess trolley" (his mother had one). I have friends who live in council estates and friends who live in castles, friends who frequent shoots and friends who frequent areas in which there are shoot-outs.

Someone recently told me that I sounded "like a moron" and should rectify my Brummie g's in "singing". Yet I am satirised for the queenly vowels with which I pronounce the word "boat". One editor, a north London public schoolboy, told me I was "too posh" for his organ. I was

forced to point out that I am merely not mockney.

And so, like most people, I fall somewhere in the middle. As in the famous sketch on *The Frost Report*, featuring Cleese, Barker and Corbett, we all tend to know where we stand. Only now, we all put ourselves in the centre. When I conducted a straw poll, everyone I asked claimed the middle ground, regardless of parentage, money, job, education and race, from lordly aristocrats to those who might once have considered themselves, like John Lennon, working-class heroes. Mind, someone did ask if I was on drugs, so unpalatable is the question. "We are all middle class now," as John Prescott declared before the 1997 election. The same John Prescott who, having once been a ship's steward, was taunted with quips such as, "Mine's a gin and tonic, Giovanni," by parliamentary peers.

Society's middle is, as surveys routinely tell us, ever more encompassing. Yet extremes certainly remain above and below. I have heard toffs use "middle-class" as a term of opprobrium (read: narrow-minded, Pooterish, provincial), just as I have witnessed them scorning people for being so déclassé as to hold jobs. When upper, middle and lower do occasionally come together – at the races, say, or political meetings – the mutual sniffiness and disdain can be palpable, allegiances unexpected.

Upper and lower share a natural affinity. As one friend, an arch social commentator, remarks, "I love how many of the upper classes behave exactly the same as the so-called underclass with reference to promiscuity, booze, drugs and general libertinage. The phrase 'The poor lad had no chance, just look at his background' could refer equally to Lord Toff d'Aristo or the scumbag son who just made his dad a grandfather aged 27. Don't quote me on this, obviously, or no one will invite me to house parties." In turn, said party throwers secretly refer to this individual as (Brideshead aristo-phile) Charles Ryder.

The different meanings invested in the term "house party" are themselves instructive. For the landed, they refer to a few days in the country, and often involve organised entertainment such as cricket or a shoot, tea, dinner and a party, and shenanigans depend upon nocturnal corridor creeping. To the "average person" such malarkey would seem fabulously Evelyn Waugh, if not latter-day Borgia, an arcane world unfolding at estates across the country of a weekend. For the middles, a "house party" translates as turning up in chinos or a wrap dress with a bottle of prosecco to stand in someone's kitchen discussing property prices. The anarchy of the toff version tends to be far more akin to riotous working-class carousing – be it drinking until comatose, lunatic drug-taking or UDIs (unidentified drinking injuries) requiring a trip to casualty – than to sedate middle-middle soirées. Middle I may be, but – call me crazy – I know where I'd rather make merry, and have the scars to prove it.

As personifications of such upper/lower affinities, I give you my friends Cam and Ron – real people, although identities have been fudged. The one lives in a "big house" in Scotland, the other in a former council house in Birmingham, both inherited from their parents, along with their contents. Both smoke and drink with abandon (as did their wives when pregnant). Both are overweight and boast "retro" illness (gout and cholesterol-indicative fat deposits about the eyes). They drive dilapidated motors and care not a jot for fashion, their clothes being weatherproof and the backs of their shoes broken down.

Both men boast relatives in the armed services. They love dogs, ignore their children, and neither they nor their offspring are university educated. Both vote Tory and admire the Royal family. Bluntness is a shared quality, while both despise the snobby niceties of the middle classes. Ron would refer to such conduct as "being ignorant". The only time I have seen Cam rage was when "a jumped-up middle-class MP was rude to a gamekeeper" or his housekeeper was over-familiar with a guest.

The form is that they hate us, while we hate ourselves, riddled by status anxiety based on a phobia of the downward social snake, with a fretful aspiration toward the upward social ladder. Outward appearances, and our fellows' judgements about them, are key. We middling types have to care about interior design because only we are compelled to create it for ourselves: everyone else is bequeathed heirlooms, or hand-me-downs. We actively engage in fashion because so much of our perceived in-groupness derives from it, whereas poshos and proles can revel in frumpery, or grotesque adornment.

We want to be seen as intelligent, fit, acceptably PC, modish, cultural, "doing well". By our buying habits you will know us, culinary not least. Witness the success of the Channel 4 show *Come Dine With Me*. Middle-classness has always been identifiable by its consumer addictions, albeit that today matters are less Betjeman's "pass the fish knives, Norman" and more "What do you mean there's no tamarind?"

The blog *The Middle Class Handbook* delights in such fetishes. Siobhan Sleet, representing its authors, the creative agency Not Actual Size, says, "Through all our fieldwork, there is one thing that has emerged as a binding force: worry. It governs every little moment in middle-class life – every thought, action and interaction. To be 'MC' is to hesitate and dither at every turn, consumed by the fear of potential social embarrassment."

Apart from self-definition via spending, the other epic source of middle-class panic is The Future. Specifically, without the carpe-diem faith that one's line will either swagger or stumble on, how bourgeois will the next generation be, not least in the age of university fees and mortgage woe? One's offspring may be a source of pride, but no less of danger.

A friend, who describes himself as "comfortable middle", denies that he is beset by the usual anxiety markers. "OK," I tell him, "what if your children were fat, stupid, mad, destined for a McJob, drug-addicted or criminal?" Immediately he twitches with horror. These things may not be pleasant for any family, but I have seen them laughed off at either end of the social spectrum, in a way that would bring a middle-class parent out in hives.

Risible though middle-class pretensions may be, at least we are culturally engaged. The yoof of *The Only Way Is Essex* and *Made In Chelsea* are not notable for their intelligence, social awareness or artistic appreciation (the latter group could not even summon the name of Sherlock Holmes's sidekick). I look back on my early years and am amazed by what I read, what I saw, the ambitiousness of the art-for-art's-sake ideals I was brought up on, and the belief that to be cultured was all.

I refuse to be ashamed of this sort of "bettering" of myself. It puts me in lofty company: Shakespeare, Wordsworth, DH Lawrence. It set me up for life – intellectually, morally and even (dread platitude) spiritually. And I hope to instil it in the young about me, to share with them the benefits of these "shallow" middle-class aspirations. If this qualifies as socially anxious, well, anxiety is a stimulus to change, progress and modernity – even if it is expressed via a vogue for chia seeds.

17 August 2014

⇨ The above information is reprinted with kind permission from *The Telegraph*. Please visit www.telegraph.co.uk for further information.

© Telegraph Media Group Limited 2015

New study shows how stereotyping holds poor children back at school

Teachers appear to assess children differently depending on their background.

By Ruby Stockham

A study published yesterday by the Institute of Education at the University of London finds that social prejudice is deeply ingrained in UK classrooms.

Researcher Tammy Campbell analysed almost 5,000 seven-year-olds at English state schools and looked at how teachers' perceptions of their ability related to their gender ethnicity and socio-economic backgrounds.

The results are striking. They show how stereotyping can impact on the assessment, and therefore on the ultimate attainment, of pupils from low-income backgrounds.

Teachers were asked to say whether individual pupils were 'well above average', 'above average', 'average', 'below average' or 'well below average' at both reading and maths. Their answers were then compared with the results of cognitive tests that the pupils had taken in the two subjects.

Some of the key findings were that:

Children from low-income families are less likely to be judged 'above average' at reading, despite having similar scores to their comparison counterparts on the reading test. Pupils from higher income families had a 52.3 per cent chance of being rated as 'above average' in reading, compared to 26.6 per cent for low-income pupils.

Children who speak other languages in addition to English are less likely to be judged 'above average' at reading than children only speaking English – despite scoring the same in the tests.

Black African and Bangladeshi pupils score relatively highly on the reading test – but are again less likely to be judged 'above average' and more likely to be judged 'below average' by their teacher.

Indian children have a 46.9 per cent chance of being judged above average at reading, compared to 28.6 per cent for Black Caribbean children.

The disparities are slightly smaller for maths; however, boys are more likely than girls to be judged 'above average' at maths (42 per cent compared to 37 per cent) inverting the general trend.

Children from families of above median income have a 45.6 per cent chance of being judged 'above average' for maths, compared to the 24.2 per cent chance of their poorer counterparts.

In general, teachers' assessments did not appear to be linked to children's ethnicity (discrepancies were mitigated by the fact that, for example, Black Caribbean children did score lower on the reading test that Indian children).

But even once other characteristics were taken into account, Black Caribbean girls tended to be under-rated in reading and maths, while Pakistani girls were more likely to be under-rated in reading and Bangladeshi boys' maths skills were more likely to be over-rated.

Commenting on her findings, Campbell said:

"Unless these tendencies are addressed, they may continue to play some part in creating and perpetuating inequalities."

It is difficult to measure the point at which a perceived lack of ability becomes actual, through lack of attention or aspiration. But we know that socio-economic background has a huge effect on pupils' performance.

A report by the Joseph Rowntree Foundation released in April found that pupils who receive free school meals do significantly worse at school. Of those eligible for free school meals in 2013/14, 63 per cent did not achieve at least five GCSEs A* to C (including English and maths) compared to 35.8 per cent of pupils not eligible for free school meals.

Campbell's report also seems to bolster the claims of the Education Committee that income background has more of an impact on underachievement than race and ethnicity. They found that just 32 per cent of poor white British children achieve five good GCSEs including English and mathematics. That figure is 42 per cent for black Caribbean children eligible for free school meals, and 61 per cent for disadvantaged Indian children.

Campbell stressed that the findings were in no way designed to condemn teachers, who are equally exposed to society's stereotyping and therefore can be expected to hold the same social biases as the rest of the public.

But she suggested that even well-meaning attempts to give disadvantaged children a better chance actually make the problem worse; for example, initiatives aimed at ethnic minority children may create the idea that these pupils are less able.

10 June 2015

⇨ The above information is reprinted with kind permission from Left Foot Forward. Please visit www.leftfootforward.org for further information.

© Left Food Forward 2015

⇨ 'Hyacinth Bucket' – the snob with working class roots in *Keeping Up Appearances*, forever trying to inflate her social status.

We find that the politics of the two crossover groups are driven far more by their 'subjective' than their 'objective' social class. Indeed, if anything, their attachment to their favoured party is slightly stronger than those whose 'subjective' and 'objective' locations are the same. Thus the Tory lead among Britain's Hyacinth Buckets is higher than among its Captain Mainwarings, while Labour does slightly better among the Dave Sparts than the Alf Garnetts – which, I suspect is precisely what the creators of these characters would predict if they all got together. And it will come as no surprise to them that Britain's Alf Garnetts – the C2DE folk who regard themselves as working class – provide more fertile ground for Ukip than any other group.

So: social class still plays a significant role in British politics; but how? Half a century ago, class experiences, loyalties and attitudes were rooted in ideology. Most working-class voters wanted more nationalisation, strong trade unions, ambitious public spending programmes and higher income taxes (which largely came from people with middle-class jobs). That was why they voted Labour. The middle classes generally had little enthusiasm for any of these things

(although, until Margaret Thatcher, few wanted to turn the clock back to small-government laissez-faire) and voted Conservative.

What are today's political dividing lines between the classes? We listed 17 policy ideas and asked people whether they agreed or disagreed with each. We were looking not so much for the overall balance of support for each policy, but for the extent to which 'middle-class' and 'working-class' voters differ.

The widest gulf concerns immigration. A big majority of 'working-class' voters want it stopped completely; 'middle-class' voters are evenly divided. Working class voters are also significantly more likely than middle-class voters to distrust MPs as a whole, to think that Britain has changed for the worse in the past 20–30 years and to want the death penalty for those who kill police officers.

The notable thing about those dividing-line issues is that they are all cultural rather than ideological. On these, class divisions are far narrower. Big majorities on both sides of the class divide support renationalisation of Britain's railways – and oppose a bigger role for private companies in the NHS. Both groups are divided on the trade-off between taxes and public spending, on whether trade unions have done more harm than good, and on whether most

recipients of welfare benefits really need the money.

There are bigger differences on the more specific issue of business leaders. Working-class voters are far more critical of their motives and their ability to command million-plus salaries. Concerns for equity (or, if you prefer, the politics of envy) still have a class dimension. But even these can be regarded as cultural more than ideological matters.

However, on two other cultural issues, there is no class gap at all: middle and working-class voters are equally divided on the decriminalising the possession of small amounts of cannabis – and majorities of both groups want to keep the new law permitting gay marriage.

This analysis helps to explain one of the big political trends of the past 60 years – the declining dominance of the two big, ideologically-rooted, parties, and the rise of the Liberal Democrats, the Greens, the Scottish National Party – and, now, Ukip.

At the time of writing, the votes in the European Parliament elections have yet to be cast; but, for a second successive election, it looks as if the combined Labour and Conservative vote will be less than 50% of all votes cast. True, this is a second-order, low-turnout election in which people feel able to cast a protest vote without risk. But it does underline how both Labour and the Tories have struggled to keep pace with the changes in British society.

Those who believe that either social class still matters in the traditional way, or doesn't matter at all, are both wrong. Social class is still a significant factor in British politics, but the nature of that factor has changed utterly. In this, as in so much else, the past is truly another country.

9 June 2014

⇨ The above information is reprinted with kind permission from YouGov. Please visit www.yougov.co.uk for further information.

© 2000-2015 YouGov plc

Self-identified social class

% support for Labour and the Conservative party among voters who consider themselves working class or middle class

Working class

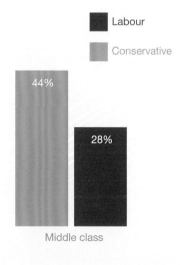

Middle class

■ Labour

■ Conservative

Source: The changing politics of social class, YouGov, 9 June 2014

Class action: the age-old divides in British society show no sign of disappearing...

... but that is not a cause for defeatism.

At first glance, the report from the Social Mobility and Child Poverty Commission contains few surprises. After all, do we really need the UK's official monitor of progress in making the country a fairer place to tell us it's unfair?

Three of the highest offices in the land are held by men who attended Eton and Oxbridge. The Mayor of London went to Eton and Oxford, the Prime Minister went to Eton and Oxford, the Archbishop of Canterbury went to Eton and Cambridge. The Cabinet, as we know, is stuffed full of alumni of fee-paying schools and Oxford and Cambridge. There is, then, little shattering about 'Elitist Britain?'

Nevertheless, the watchdog's study is a profoundly disturbing document, painting a bleak picture of a nation that likes to think it has shaken off the class-ridden strictures of the past but is in deep hock to them still. In the higher echelons of public life – whether it's the judiciary, armed forces, Whitehall, BBC, even the England cricket and rugby teams – a small elite is wildly over-represented. Just seven per cent of the public as a whole attend independent schools, yet 71 per cent of our top judges did so, 62 per cent of our senior military officers, and 55 per cent of civil service permanent secretaries.

How can it possibly be right that in this so-called modern, inclusive country, one in seven judges went to just five independent schools? Neither is it so simple a matter as a right-wing ruling establishment looking after its own: 22 per cent of the Shadow Cabinet went to private school against that seven per cent national figure. The divide goes on, through the media and business. In a year's guests on BBC's *Question Time*, 43 per cent of them were ex-Oxbridge and 37 per cent attended fee-paying schools.

These aren't throwaway statistics to be revisited in gentle TV comedies about class – they are extremely real and raise serious questions. How can professions and public bodies begin to have any understanding of the people they profess to serve when they're so heavily comprised of representatives from identical backgrounds? We like to boast that Britain is more meritocratic and egalitarian than it once was, a worthy competitor in the 21st-century global marketplace, but those words ring hollow when confronted with these findings.

Our leaders argue passionately for greater social mobility, but, as this study finds, they surround themselves with colleagues who experienced similar cloistered schools and colleges. Set against 'Elitist Britain?', genuine social mobility in the UK is but a figment of the fertile imagination of a senior politician or mandarin (Eton and Oxford, probably).

Worryingly, there is little sign of change. In 2012, only 25 recruits to the Civil Service Fast Stream, out of more than 600, were from working-class backgrounds. Strides have been made in public life to open up opportunities to women and ethnic minorities. The same approach has to be taken towards class. If that means positive selection on class grounds then so be it. All the advantages that those at the top take for granted must be tackled, such as open-ended unpaid internships. Instead, we need increased availability of funding for postgraduate education; schools to provide greater extra-curricular activities and ensure their pupils receive excellent careers advice and access to networks; universities to take a rounder view of a candidate; and employers to widen their talent pools. One intriguing proposal is for recruiters to seek university-blind applications, so no mention is made anywhere of a candidate's alma mater.

This, and more, has to be followed if Britain is to truly change. Make no mistake: while we ponder, countries that are not so hidebound are powering ahead.

28 August 2014

⇨ The above information is reprinted with kind permission from *The Independent*. Please visit www.independent.co.uk for further information.

I couldn't put him in front of a client. He'd show me up!

© independent.co.uk 2015

Facebook data suggests people from higher social class have fewer international friends

New study using Facebook network data, including a dataset of over 57 billion friendships, shows correlation between higher social class and fewer international friendships. Researchers say results support ideas of 'restricting social class' among wealthy, but show that lower social classes are taking advantage of increased social capital beyond national borders.

A new study conducted in collaboration with Facebook using anonymised data from the social networking site shows a correlation between people's social and financial status, and the levels of internationalism in their friendship networks – with those from higher social classes around the world having fewer friends outside of their own country.

Despite the fact that, arguably, people from higher social classes should be better positioned to travel and meet people from different countries, researchers found that, when it comes to friendship networks, people from those groups had lower levels of internationalism and made more friends domestically than abroad.

Researchers say that their results are in line with what's known as the 'restricting social class' hypothesis: that high-social class individuals have greater resources, and therefore depend less on others – with the wealthy tending to be less socially engaged, particularly with those from groups other than their own, as a result.

The research team, from the Prosociality and Well-Being Lab in the University of Cambridge's Department of Psychology, conducted two studies – one local and one global, with the global study using a dataset of billions of Facebook friendships – and the results from both supported the idea of restricting social class.

However, the researchers say the fact that those of lower social status tend to have more international connections demonstrates how low-social class people "may actually stand to benefit most from a highly international and globalised social world".

"The findings point to the possibility that the wealthy stay more in their own social bubble, but this is unlikely to be ultimately beneficial. If you are not engaging internationally then you will miss out on that international resource – that flow of new ideas and information," said co-author Dr Aleksandr Spectre, who heads up the lab.

"The results could also be highlighting a mechanism of how the modern era might facilitate a closing of the inequality gap, as those from lower social classes take advantage of platforms like Facebook to increase their social capital beyond national borders," he said.

For the first study, the 'local', the team recruited 857 people in the United States and asked them to self-report their perceived social status (from working to upper class on a numerical scale), as well as an objective indicator in the form of annual household income. The volunteers also provided researchers access to their Facebook networks.

The results from the first study indicated that low-social class people have nearly 50% more international friends than high-social class people.

For the second study, the 'global', the team approached Facebook directly, who provided data on every friendship formed over the network in every country in the world at the national aggregate level for 2011. All data was anonymous. The dataset included over 57 billion friendships.

The research team quantified social class on a national level based on each country's economic standing by using gross domestic product (GDP) per capita data for 2011 as published by the World Bank.

After controlling for as many variables as they were able, the researchers again found a negative correlation between social class – this time on a national level – and the percentage of Facebook friends from other countries. For people from low-social class countries, 35% of their friendships on average were international, compared to 28% average in high-social class countries.

The findings from the two studies provide support for the restricting social class hypothesis on both a local and a global level, say the researchers. The results are contained in a new paper, published in the journal *Personality and Individual Differences*.

"Previous research by others has highlighted the value of developing weak ties to people in distant social circles, because they offer access to resources not likely to be found in one's immediate circle. I find it encouraging that low-social class people tend to have greater access to these resources on account of having more international friendships," said co-author Maurice Yearwood.

"From a methodological perspective, this combination of micro and macro starts to build a very interesting initial story. These are just correlations at the moment, but it's a fascinating start for this type of research going forward," Yearwood said.

Spectre says that the high levels of Facebook usage and sheer size of the network makes it a "pretty good proxy for your social environment. The vast majority of Facebook friendships are ones where people have met in person and engaged with each other, a lot of the properties you find in Facebook friendship networks will strongly mirror everyday life," he said.

"We are entering an era with big data and social media where we can start to ask really big questions and gain answers to them in a way we just couldn't do before. I think this research is a good example of that, I don't know how we could even have attempted this work ten years ago," Spectre said.

The latest work is the first output of ongoing research collaborations between Spectre's lab in Cambridge and Facebook, a company he commends for its "scientific spirit".

"Having the opportunity to work with companies like Facebook, Twitter, Microsoft and Google should be something that's hugely exciting to the academic community," he said.

Reference

Yearwood, M. H., Cuddy, A., Lamba, N., Youyou, W., van der Lowe, I., Piff, P., Gronin, C., Fleming, P., Simon-Thomas, E., Keltner, D., & Spectre, A. (2015). On wealth and the diversity of friendships: High social class people around the world have fewer international friends. Personality and Individual Differences, 87, 224-229. DOI: doi:10.1016/j.paid.2015.07.040

10 September 2015

⇨ The above information is reprinted with kind permission from the University of Cambridge. Please visit www.cam.ac.uk for further information.

© 2015 University of Cambridge

Global middle class nears one billion mark

According to the most recent Allianz Global Wealth Report, the global middle class is nearing the billion people mark. Significant inequalities though remain in many countries, and data shows important differences within the world's regions.

The global gross financial assets – namely securities, bank deposits, and claims on insurance and pensions – of private households grew by 9.9% in 2013, the highest rate of growth since 2003. This brought total global financial assets up to a new record level of €118 trillion.

"The share of the population that falls into the wealthy middle class has doubled in Latin America, has almost trebled in eastern Europe and has increased seven-fold in Asia"

Switzerland, the USA and Belgium are the top-three countries in the world when it comes to net per capita financial assets.

Since the end of 2000, the proportion of global gross financial assets that is attributable to North America and western Europe has fallen by 6%, yet both regions still account for a combined total of almost 70% of the global asset base. In other words, more than four-fifths of global financial assets are still in the hands of private households living in the world's richer areas, even though these households make up 18.8% of the Earth's population.

Growth in wealth has been particularly strong in eastern Europe (especially among non-EU members). Over the past 13 years, only Asia's emerging markets have grown more quickly. While Latin America has slowed down – in 2013, asset growth dropped to 6.4%, compared with 13.5% in 2012, and well below the emerging market average (+17.1%).

Global middle class nearing one billion mark

One of the most interesting sections in the report is on the growth of a global middle class – which is now nearing the one-billion mark. Allianz defines this "wealth middle class" by taking the average global net per capita financial assets (€17,700 in 2013), as a basis, and then encompasses all individuals with assets corresponding to somewhere between 30% and 180% of this figure.

The flows between wealth classes are particularly interesting. The middle class includes both 65 million people that have been demoted from the "wealth upper class" since 2000, and 491 million new entrants.

The share of the population that falls into the wealth middle class in global terms has doubled in Latin America, has almost trebled in eastern Europe and has increased seven-fold in Asia.

While the number of members of the lower wealth class has remained relatively constant at around 3.5 billion people – this, in part at least, is likely to be explained by population growth.

Within each region though there are important differences. The Allianz report includes a series of charts to show how equality (or inequality in several cases) is evolving.

In Latin America, developments have been by and large positive, with the exception of Colombia, where wealth distribution hasn't basically changed since 2000. The picture is far more mixed in Asia, with conditions improving in countries like Thailand and Malaysia, not changing or getting worse in already unequal Indonesia and India, and deteriorating in Japan, which was once one of the world's most equal countries.

The wealth matrix in eastern European is quite uniform – with one major exception: Russia, which already had noticeable wealth differences, and these are now widening further.

Finally, in terms of Europe, North America and Oceania, the USA remains by far the most elitist among the countries analysed in the report. While wealth distribution, has broadly speaking become more

equal, or remains unchanged, in most countries since 2000, it is worth noting how in Greece, Ireland, Italy and France the proportion of assets attributable to the more wealthy decile has increased considerably.

The complete *Allianz Global Wealth Report* can be found. The sections on growing private debt in Asia, and the growth in real estate assets (and liabilities) in the UK

and eastern Europe are particularly recommended.

24 September 2014

⇨ The above information is reprinted with kind permission from *The Guardian*. Please visit www.theguardian.com for further information.

© 2015 Guardian News and Media Limited

Why are middle-class people more likely to play music, paint and act?

Press release from the British Sociological Association.

The reason why middle-class people are more likely to play music, paint and act has been revealed in a major new study.

Research involving 78,000 people found that it was not wealth or social status that were strongly linked to people taking part in arts activities as amateurs or professionals.

Instead, it was the level of education that lay behind arts participation, the study by Dr Aaron Reeves, a sociologist at the University of Oxford, found.

In an article in the journal *Sociology*, Dr Reeves said that of the 78,011 surveyed, 18% had taken part in painting or photography, 9% in dance, 10% in music, 2% in drama or opera; 6% had written poetry, plays or fiction. Only 22% had not done any artistic activities.

He found that having a higher income did not make arts participation more likely – those earning over £30,000 a year were less likely to take part than those earning less.

Social status mattered little – those in higher professional jobs were less likely to take part in the arts than those in lower professional jobs, and only slightly more likely to take part than those in lower supervisory roles and semi-routine roles.

Instead, the clearest link with artistic activity was education. After accounting for the influence of family class background by statistical analysis, he found that those with

a degree were around four times more likely to take part in painting and photography than those with no educational qualification, five times more likely to be involved in dance and in crafts, and four times more likely to play a musical instrument.

Those taking part in arts were more likely to be middle class, simply because they were more likely to be highly educated. But although having a middle class background makes it more likely that someone had gone to university, Dr Reeves's findings showed that they were no more likely to take part in arts after graduating than were working-class students.

Dr Reeves said that results for arts participation were different from those for watching or listening to arts performances, where social class and status were strongly linked to higher rates of arts consumption.

"Arts participation, unlike arts consumption and cultural engagement generally, is not closely associated with either social class or social status," said Dr Reeves in the article. "This result deviates from the expectation – unexpectedly, those with higher incomes are less likely to be arts participants.

"These results show that it is educational attainment alone, and not social status, that is shaping the probability of being an arts participant."

Dr Reeves suggests two reasons for the link with education. "First, those

with higher information processing capacity are more likely to enjoy highbrow cultural practices, such as arts participation, and be university graduates. In short, university graduates are more likely to possess the cultural resources necessary for both arts consumption and arts participation.

"Second, universities make admissions decisions using information on extracurricular and cultural activities, increasing the likelihood that university graduates are culturally active."

Sociology is published by the British Sociological Association and SAGE

16 September 2015

⇨ *The reason why middle class people are more likely to play music, paint and act revealed by research*, 2015, British Sociological Association, http:// www.britsoc.co.uk/media/90187/ The_reason_why_middle_class_ people_are_more_likely_to_play_ music_paint_and_act_revealed_ by_research_PR150915. pdf?1444659611803.

⇨ The British Sociological Association is both a registered charity (no. 1080235) and a company limited by guarantee (no. 3890729).

© British Sociological Association 2015

Social class and its influence on health

While individuals' socioeconomic status is the most significant social influence on health and well-being, wealth distribution through society as a whole also plays a part.

By David Matthews

Five key points

⇨ There is an established link between poverty and poor health

⇨ Insecure, poorly paid employment has been shown to have a detrimental impact on health and well-being

⇨ The most important materialistic influences on health are diet, housing, working conditions, exposure to pollution, the urban environment and public services

⇨ Economic inequalities lead to inequalities in health and well-being

⇨ Being encouraged to strive for wealth negatively affects mental well-being and happiness

Variations in health and well-being across the UK are significantly influenced by social and economic inequality, which is largely indicated by occupation and income or, more broadly, social class. There is an established link between low income and poor health, and a definitive correlation between health and occupation, with insecure, poorly paid work having a detrimental impact on health and well-being (Marmot et al, 2010). Indeed, much research into socioeconomic health inequalities uses occupational classifications to demonstrate inequality.

Friedrich Engels recognised the link between occupation and health in the mid-Victorian era (Engels,1845, reprinted 2009) and showed infant mortality was far higher in the working than in the upper classes. This inequality has not been eradicated: between 1982 and 2006 health inequalities between occupational groups increased.

Illustrating the social gradient of health – health status worsens as you go down the socioeconomic scale – between 1982 and 1986, life expectancy for men in Class 1 was 2.3 and 4.9 years greater than those in Classes 3 and 7 respectively. By 2002–2006, although the gap between Classes 1 and 3 had declined to 1.9 years, that between Classes 1 and 7 had increased to 5.8 years (Office for National Statistics, 2011).

Materialism and life conditions

Preoccupation with socioeconomic status is known as materialism (Bartley, 2004); it is relevant to nurses because individuals' material existence can reduce or enhance their health. This was established by the Black report (Black et al, 1980), which exposed the extent of health inequalities in Britain, but current understanding of this approach to health has its origins in the work of Engels (1845, reprinted 2009). Ill health was seen as the result of the capitalist pursuit of profit at the expense of the working classes, most of whom worked in dangerous conditions that often caused illness and disability, and lived in overcrowded places that made it easy for disease to spread.

White (2013) stated that the most significant materialist influences on health are:

⇨ Diet;

⇨ Housing;

⇨ Working conditions;

⇨ Exposure to pollution;

⇨ Organisation of the urban landscape.

Another important factor influencing health inequality is the provision – or lack – of public services (Bartley, 2004). The unequal distribution of income determines the relationship between individuals and these factors: those on the lowest income are likely to be most adversely affected by lack of public services.

Diet and housing

People on lower incomes are likely to buy goods and services that negatively affect their health (Marmot et al, 2010). Poor diet, often portrayed as the result of a lack of education, is often the result of a lack of money to buy nutritious food.

Housing is overwhelmingly determined by level of income and can significantly impact on health. Poorer housing increases the risk of accidents due to overcrowding and unsafe conditions, while damp, poor air quality leads to a higher risk of respiratory problems (White, 2013).

Working conditions

Working conditions also significantly influence health. Globally, 350,000 people die each year due to workplace accidents (Mathers et al, 2009) and the physical nature of work can have serious consequences. For example, 37% of all back pain is due to occupational factors (Mathers et al, 2009), while jobs that expose workers to hazardous chemicals, substances and airborne particles can lead to asbestosis and silicosis; such conditions are often found in manual labour jobs. However, occupations in the middle of the scale can also negatively affect health: white-collar roles expose workers to greater risk of repetitive strain injury and sedentary conditions.

Occupation can also affect the mental health of different groups in different ways. People at the lower end of the socioeconomic scale may feel a lack of control or autonomy at work, resulting in a sense of alienation, which has a negative effect on their mental well-being, while more senior white-collar roles may lead to high levels of stress, which can also negatively affect mental well-being and increase the risk of cardiovascular disease.

The urban environment

The built environment can also affect socioeconomic inequalities and have serious consequences on health. A locality's economic status affects physical features, resources and the socio-cultural environment (Annandale, 2014). The affluence or poverty of an urban area influences the availability of public services, housing conditions, pollution levels, crime rates and the quality of private sector enterprises in terms of the goods and services provided.

Between 2010 and 2012, life expectancy for women born in Dorset (relatively affluent) was 86.6 years, compared with 78.5 years in Glasgow (relatively deprived); men aged 65 in Harrow (relatively affluent) could expect to live for another 20.9 years versus 14.9 years in Glasgow (ONS, 2014).

There are even greater variations in the length of time people can expect to live in good health. For 2010–12, healthy life expectancy for men was highest in Richmond upon Thames (affluent) at 70.0 years versus 52.5 years in Tower Hamlets (relatively deprived) (ONS, 2014). This means males in the most affluent London borough can expect 17.5 more years of healthy life than those in the most deprived.

The Royal Society for Public Health (2015) highlights the impact of the urban landscape on health in its definition of a healthy town. To promote good health, healthy towns require high streets that are:

⇨ Free from excess noise and pollution;

⇨ Architecturally designed to support activities such as walking and cycling;

⇨ Planned to provide services that allow social interaction, improving social cohesion;

⇨ Designed to encourage the establishment of businesses providing healthier services and goods.

Crucially, the research identified a link between healthy high streets and local deprivation, with the localities of the ten unhealthiest high streets exhibiting greater levels of deprivation than those of the ten healthiest (RSPH, 2015).

More equal and healthier

So far it has been argued that low income and material deprivation can have severe health consequences. However, it is increasingly argued that health inequalities are not just related to level of income, but that large inequalities of wealth within society in general have a negative effect on health. Economic inequality in Britain has increased dramatically over the last three decades (Annandale, 2014). This can have potentially adverse effects on individuals' health – Wilkinson (2005) argued that the least health inequalities are seen in cultures with the smallest income differentials and greater social cohesion.

The social gradient of health is influenced by the existence of relative deprivation. The poorer health of middle-income earners relative to the most affluent is less to do with the absolute amount of income they earn than with their perceived lack of material possessions relative to others, and their anxiety to achieve greater social status.

Consumer goods, including housing, are often given a symbolic value, which is thought to reflect the worth of those who possess them. It could be argued that the pursuit of ever-more material goods encourages people to become dissatisfied with their present material circumstances, demonstrating envy and mistrust towards others, reducing social cohesion and having negative consequences, in particular on mental well-being and happiness.

If health inequalities are to be seriously reduced, society must invest in individuals and environments where deprivation, poverty and economic insecurity are common. An individual's health and well-being cannot be reduced to genetics, biology or poor lifestyle choices; it is the result of social inequalities (Marmot et al, 2010). Further, it is clear that a society that values materialist acquisitions as representations of success breeds division. It could be argued that a healthy society is one built on equality, social justice and social cohesion.

References

Annandale E (2014) *The Sociology of Health and Medicine: A Critical Introduction.* Cambridge: Polity Press.

Bartley M (2004) *Health Inequality: An Introduction to Theories, Concepts and Methods.* Cambridge: Polity Press.

Black D et al (1980) *Inequalities in Health: Report of a Research Working Group.* London: Department of Health and Social Security.

Engels F (1845) *The Condition of the Working Class in England.* London: Penguin, 2009 reprint.

Marmot M et al (2010) *Fair Society, Healthy Lives: The Marmot Review.*

Mathers C et al (2009) *Global Health Risks: Mortality and Burden of Disease Attributable to Major Risks.*

Office for National Statistics (2014) *Healthy Life Expectancy at Birth for Upper Tier Local Authorities: England, 2010-12.*

Office for National Statistics (2011) *Trends in Life Expectancy by the National Statistics Socio-Economic Classification 1982-2006.*

Royal Society for Public Health (2015) *Health on the High Street.*

White K (2013) *An Introduction to the Sociology of Health and Illness.* London: Sage Publications.

Wilkinson RG (2005) *Unhealthy Societies: The Afflictions of Inequality.* Abingdon: Routledge.

12 October 2015

⇨ The above information is reprinted with kind permission from *Nursing Times*. Please visit www.nursingtimes.net for further information.

⇨ Please note that this article is not for further distribution and Emap Publishing Ltd remains the owner of the copyright.

© *Nursing Times/Emap Publishing Ltd 2015*

'Shocking' inequality levels in Britain must be addressed, says John Major

Former Conservative Prime Minister wants to see greater concentration on people failed by the system.

By Benn Quinn

Former Conservative Prime Minister Sir John Major has criticised the "shocking" impact of inequality in Britain and said more needed to be done to urgently tackle the gap between the rich and the poor.

In a speech reiterating a number of touchstones of one-nation Conservatism, he pointedly set himself against language that sought to cast those who were out of work as "idlers" and benefit claimants as "scroungers".

Delivering a Hinton lecture entitled 'A nation at ease with itself?', Major told the audience in London that he had begun to reflect more and more on inequality as he grew older.

In a country now immensely more wealthy than the one in which he grew up, he said that life was still not easy for many, adding: "Even in areas that are recognised as wealthy, there are families or individuals who have fallen behind.

"Policymakers must understand how hard it is to escape from such circumstances. It is not inertia that keeps the unemployed immobile: it is simply that, without help, they are trapped."

Turning to the role of the benefits system, he said: "Let us cast aside a common misconception. Everyone out of work is not an idler.

"Everyone in receipt of benefits is not a scrounger. Of course idlers and scroungers exist – and governments are entirely right to root out the cheats who rip off the taxpayer. But the focus must not be only on those who abuse the system; we need equal concentration on those who are failed by the system."

Describing poverty as being "not only about empty pockets", Major described contemporary Britain as one in which the lifespan of the poorest in some major cities was 20 years shorter than those of the most wealthy.

"I have no doubt that much of this disparity is caused by poor lifestyle, poor choices, poor diet – but poor environment, poor housing and poor education must surely be contributory factors. Whatever the reasons, this is a shocking situation in 2015," he added.

The former Prime Minister went on to deliver a plea for the upgrade of Britain's infrastructure, as well as emphasising the roles of the private sector and charities.

However, while talking of his pride in the scale of philanthropic, voluntary and charitable work across the UK, Major warned that a reality check was required, stating: "We cannot be complacent about our charitable sector. There are negatives: we have all seen the publicity generated by bad fund raising practices and poor governance.

"I won't dwell on these shortcomings, except to note that all charities have a duty to protect their reputation. Unless they are seen as efficient and well run, donations will fall away."

11 November 2015

⇨ The above information is reprinted with kind permission from *The Guardian*. Please visit www.theguardian.com for further information.

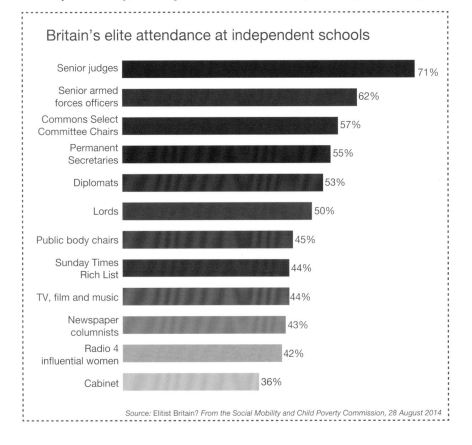

Britain's elite attendance at independent schools

Senior judges	71%
Senior armed forces officers	62%
Commons Select Committee Chairs	57%
Permanent Secretaries	55%
Diplomats	53%
Lords	50%
Public body chairs	45%
Sunday Times Rich List	44%
TV, film and music	44%
Newspaper columnists	43%
Radio 4 influential women	42%
Cabinet	36%

Source: Elitist Britain? From the Social Mobility and Child Poverty Commission, 28 August 2014

© 2015 Guardian News and Media Limited

Social mobility

There is more social mobility in more equal societies.

People may move up or down the social ladder within their lifetime or from one generation to the next. That everyone has the same chance of moving up is what lies behind the idea of equality of opportunity.

One way to measure social mobility is to see whether rich parents have rich children and poor parents poor children, or whether the incomes of parents and their children are unrelated. Can children of poor parents become rich? Researchers at the London School of Economics have used this method to compare social mobility in eight countries. Using their data, we have shown that, at least among these few countries, the more equal countries have higher social mobility. It looks as if the American Dream is far more likely to remain a dream for Americans than it is for people living in Scandinavian countries. Greater inequalities of outcome seem to make it easier for rich parents to pass on their advantages. While income differences have widened in Britain and the USA, social mobility has slowed. Bigger income differences may make it harder to achieve equality of opportunity because they increase social class differentiation and perhaps prejudice.

More Information

Wilkinson RG, Pickett KE. The problems of relative deprivation: why some societies do better than others. *Social Science and Medicine* 2007; 65: 1965-78.

Blanden J, Gregg P, Machin S. Intergenerational mobility in Europe and North America. London: Centre for Economic Performance, London School of Economics, 2005.

Wilkinson RG, Pickett KE. *The Spirit Level*. Penguin. 2009. Buy the book from Amazon.

⇨ The above information is reprinted with kind permission from The Equality Trust. Please visit www.equalitytrust.org.uk for further information.

© *The Equality Trust 2015*

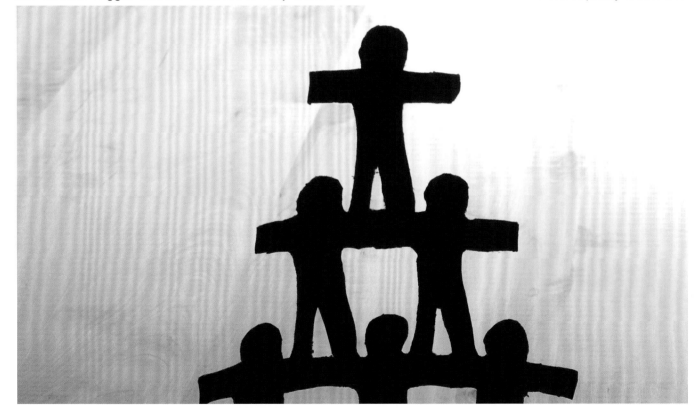

Social mobility a problem – but no agreement on solutions

There is a clear feeling among British people that success is more to do with class and connections than talent – but there is resistance to both left- and right-leaning solutions.

By Will Dahlgreen

Former Conservative Prime Minister John Major recently attacked what he called the "truly shocking" fact that "In every single sphere of British influence, the upper echelons of power in 2013 are held overwhelmingly by the privately educated or the affluent middle class." Though his attack was directed at Labour, his comments were viewed as a challenge to David Cameron, whose Cabinet is 62% private and two-thirds Oxbridge educated.

YouGov research from earlier this year finds significant unrest among the British public over the difficulty for ordinary people to move through society's ranks. However, the unease is counterbalanced by resistance to many proposed solutions.

The majority of British adults (56%) say senior professions are unfairly dominated by people from affluent middle-class backgrounds. 31% say they are open to people of all backgrounds.

By 44%–32%, British society is felt to have become less mobile in the last 30 years.

And 48% say knowing the right people and having the right connections is most likely to bring people career success, while 32% pin it down to getting a good education and 16% say it is due to innate abilities and talents.

However, the two most commonly proposed measures to counterbalance this problem – one on the left and one on the right of the political spectrum – are both met with resistance.

One proposal is positive discrimination: lowering university entry requirements for those from backgrounds where the odds are stacked against them. 49% oppose this while 29% support it.

An alternative is more selective education: creating grammar schools allowed to select the brightest pupils from any background and give them a better chance. 46% oppose creating more of these or closing existing ones,

while 37% say there should be more. In fact, support for creating more grammar schools appears to be dropping slightly since June.

Both Conservative and Labour governments dismantled grammar schools from the late sixties onwards – either replacing them with fee-paying or comprehensive institutions. There now remain 164 grammar schools in Britain, but despite some championing them as a solution to social immobility they remain middle-class institutions: while 18% of state school pupils are on free school meals, at grammar schools only 3% are.

12 November 2013

⇨ The above information is reprinted with kind permission from YouGov. Please visit www.yougov.co.uk for further information.

© 2000-2015 YouGov plc

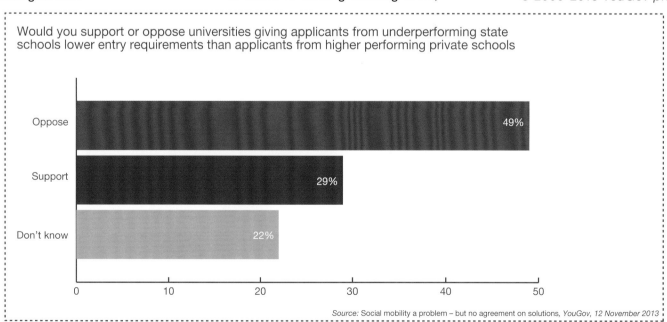

Would you support or oppose universities giving applicants from underperforming state schools lower entry requirements than applicants from higher performing private schools

- Oppose: 49%
- Support: 29%
- Don't know: 22%

Source: Social mobility a problem – but no agreement on solutions, *YouGov, 12 November 2013*

Social mobility and the City: does everyone get a fair chance with graduate recruiters?

A look at the effectiveness and the justice of graduate recruitment in the City.

By Hannah Langworth

What is social mobility and why should it matter to you? Social mobility is about your right to embark on the career path of your choice and progress as far as you want to, subject only to your abilities and ambitions. Whether your peers can do the same also affects you – organisations with a mix of people with different backgrounds and experiences function better, and offer their employees richer working lives.

However, *Elitist Britain*, a report published earlier this year by the Social Mobility and Child Poverty Commission, states: "The sheer scale of the dominance of certain backgrounds [in influential and prestigious professional roles in the UK] raises questions about the degree to which the composition of the elite reflects merit.

"Access to top jobs and opportunities should not be dependent on where you come

from," the report adds. We agree, so we're taking a look at City and business careers and social mobility in a series of articles: what the problems are, why they matter, and what employers are doing to combat them. In this article, the focus is on the first part of any career: recruitment.

What's going wrong

"The best people need to be in the best jobs; in a truly meritocratic society, employers recruit people on their aptitude, competence and potential for a certain role," says the *Elitist Britain* report.

But, says Lee Elliot Major of the Sutton Trust, an organisation that works to improve social mobility, graduate recruitment in the UK today is falling short of this ideal: "The evidence and research we've commissioned and that others have done [shows] that the barriers to social mobility are increasing. There's a huge amount of talent out there that we're not exploiting.

Both Lee and the Elitist Britain report identify not attending a highly-ranked university and not having access to careers information and assistance as factors unfairly holding some candidates back in the recruitment process.

Lawyer Chris White, who left his job in the City to found diversity organisation Aspiring Solicitors, experienced these kinds of difficulties when trying to get started on a legal career, being from a low-income and non-professional family, state-educated, and someone not studying at a highly-ranked university.

"Through the application process I came across a number of barriers and discrimination," Chris says. However, while he encountered some direct prejudice against his background, he points out that barriers and discrimination in the City's graduate recruitment processes can also take the form

OF THE WEALTHIEST 100 UK-BORN PEOPLE IN THE TV, FILM AND MUSIC INDUSTRIES...

44 % attended Independent Schools

28% attended Grammar Schools

24% attended Comprehensive School

52% attended a University

31% attended a Russell Group University

11% attended an Oxbridge University

Source: Elitist Britain? From the Social Mobility and Child Poverty Commission, 28 August 2014

of unconscious bias or practical limitations – for example, many employers lack the resources to target as many universities as they would like, so they concentrate on those at the top of the league tables and thereby miss some excellent potential candidates.

What the City is getting right

Efforts are being made, however, to ensure that top students and graduates from every background get the opportunities they deserve to start their careers in the City.

Social mobility organisations, including the Sutton Trust, run a number of programmes designed to encourage top students from all backgrounds to go for City graduate jobs. All university students interested in a career in law can join Aspiring Solicitors, which runs commercial awareness sessions, employer presentations and networking events.

City employers are playing their part too. Many are targeting students from a wider range of universities than they did in the past. Some employers are working with the Sutton Trust, Aspiring Solicitors and other organisations to spread information about their graduate opportunities further, educate their recruiters about unconscious bias, and generally make their recruitment processes fairer.

It's also worth noting that City employers here have a better track record than those in the UK's other elite professional sectors on fair graduate recruitment processes in some respects, having generally never used unpaid internships extensively or required graduates to pay for essential postgraduate training themselves, two areas that were highlighted in *Elitist Britain* as particularly problematic in social mobility terms.

Show your potential and be proud of who you are

There are a few particularly interesting and encouraging steps being taken by City and business employers to make their recruitment processes fairer that you might encounter.

Some financial institutions and professional services firms, including global bank BNP Paribas and KMPG, are using online skills-based games as ways of engaging with and assessing the potential of students that might not have access to traditional recruitment channels and opportunities.

Meanwhile, in the legal sector, international law firm Clifford Chance is a good example of an employer moving firmly in the right direction in an innovative way, having recently won awards in the social mobility and graduate recruitment area from the

Association of Graduate Recruiters and the Black Solicitors' Network.

Among other social mobility initiatives, all recruitment for graduate places at the firm is done on a CV-blind basis – that is, applicant CVs are not given to interviewers in advance in order to prevent them making snap judgements about applicants on the basis of their background, education, career history or interests. The measure has received a lot of media attention and has been adopted by some other City law firms.

However, the firm does recognise that winning a place at a good university, getting high grades, work experience and other achievements typically found on a CV are significant to recruitment decisions, says Laura Yeates, Graduate Recruitment and Development Manager at the firm.

"It's not that there are certain questions that are off-bounds [in an interview]," she says. "Rather, the individual candidate provides their own narrative of their particular strengths and experiences."

This approach hints at something you can do yourself to make sure recruiters give you a fair chance: have self-belief and the confidence to pursue what you think you're capable of achieving, even if you encounter setbacks. Chris offers this advice: "Be proud of who you are and don't let anybody tell you that because you're gay, because you're black, because you're state-educated that you're not as good as somebody else.

"The only two things that a potential employer should judge you on [are] your ability and your personality and if anybody says anything outside of that, don't listen to them because they're wrong."

October 2014

⇨ The above information is reprinted with kind permission from The Gateway. Please visit www.thegatewayonline.com for further information.

© The Gateway 2015

A HELPING HAND

Education and social mobility

By Kate Hoskins, Reader in Education, University of Roehampton

Over the past two decades the UK state education system has faced increasing pressure to raise academic standards and improve outcomes for all young people, regardless of their social background and identity. The previous Coalition Government emphasised the need for a rigorous academic curriculum, with tough examinations to match. Their new academies must, they argue, emulate the best independent schools. They want students on free school meals to have similar opportunities to those at Eton or Harrow and they expect many of them to rise to the highest positions in society (HMG, 2011). In fulfilling these aims, the Government claim that social mobility through education can become a reality for the majority.

"Students often attributed their interests, hobbies and activities to family members, including parents, grandparents and other significant relatives"

To explore the likely success of the UK Government's aims and objectives to improve social mobility for England, Professor Bernard Barker and I conducted research to analyse 88 young people's thoughts and feelings about their family backgrounds, aspirations, education and future careers (Hoskins and Barker, 2014). The research participants were located in two academies with 'good' and 'outstanding' characteristics, similar to those that policy-makers wish to see adopted across the country to increase performance and mobility for everyone (HMG, 2011; DfE, 2010a). Both schools emphasise high-quality teaching, hard work and aiming high. These schools have high expectations and set demanding targets. They

are prototypes of the new academy regime, expected to emulate top independent schools despite accepting the full ability range and receiving per-pupil funding that is approximately 70 per cent less than at the average private school (Gunter, 2011).

We found that the Government's one-sided, individualist plans neglect the reality of children's lives and experience, and over-estimate the extent to which policy reforms can increase the number of young people obtaining higher-status jobs. The majority of our students presented themselves as astute, highly motivated, and hard-working. Almost all described clear plans for the future and recognised that they would have to adapt to circumstances, including unfavourable grades. They were acting as the reflexive agents of individualism whose decisions were 'pragmatically rational' (Hodkinson et al., 1996).

Despite government pressure for schools to 'overcome' family background, the students were strongly influenced by family values and culture. They often attributed their interests, hobbies and activities to family members, including parents, grandparents and other significant relatives.

Very few participants were actively striving for social mobility. Our data did not confirm the policy assumption that young people are dissatisfied with their lives and families and wish to climb the social and economic ladder. On the contrary, the most frequently voiced areas of aspiration were personal happiness and satisfaction, with family life and intrinsically rewarding work seen as more important to feelings of success and well-being than the pursuit of status and wealth.

The students are not isolated individuals in simple pursuit of ever more prestigious credentials, but contributors to evolving family patterns and networks that produce

advantages or disadvantages for successive generations.

The data suggests that academies are unlikely to overcome family background or significantly increase social mobility. Rather, they seem to embed differences in family wealth, with successful students invariably describing advantages transmitted through their parents.

Perhaps a different approach to improving social mobility is required and could encompass the following:

⇨ Further research that recognises the family, including women and girls, as the main influence on social mobility. Policy could be informed by qualitative, alongside quantitative, studies that show the ways in which young people's dispositions are formed and influenced, and help us understand how small advantages are transmitted between generations.

⇨ Provide structured support to increase the proportion of women reaching senior professional and managerial positions.

⇨ Curriculum, assessment and guidance systems could be designed to encourage all young people and to value their talents and aspirations equally, whatever they are. Excessive testing, negative examination feedback and premature tracking into academic and vocational pathways should be avoided.

26 May 2015

⇨ The above information is reprinted with kind permission from British Educational Research Association (BERA) Blog. Please visit www.bera.ac.uk/blog for further information.

© British Educational Research Association 2015

Social mobility report finds 'poshness test' applied by top firms for job applicants

By Kathryn Snowdon

Working-class applicants are being sidelined by the UK's leading firms as personal style, accent and middle-class mannerisms are frequently used to judge "talent", a social mobility report has found.

The Social Mobility and Child Poverty Commission said that leading law and accountancy firms employ workers from a small pool of graduates – many of whom went to private or selective schools or come from affluent backgrounds.

The report found that "polished" candidates stood a much better chance of securing a job at the firms, despite attempts at the companies to improve social inclusion in the past ten to 15 years.

Commission chairman Alan Milburn, the former Labour health secretary, said: "This research shows that young people with working-class backgrounds are

being systematically locked out of top jobs. Elite firms seem to require applicants to pass a 'poshness test' to gain entry.

"Inevitably that ends up excluding youngsters who have the right sort of grades and abilities but whose parents do not have the right sort of bank balances.

"Thankfully some of our country's leading firms are making a big commitment to recruit the brightest and best, regardless of background. They should be applauded. But for the rest, this is a wake up and smell the coffee moment."

When hiring new recruits, firms "continue to focus their attraction strategies on a limited number of elite universities" because it is deemed more cost effective and efficient, the report found.

Students from Russell Group universities – of which there are 24 in the UK – were more likely to be picked for the role.

Employers admitted there might be suitable candidates from other universities, but said such a search could be time consuming, so they would often "fish in certain ponds" to find new employees.

One employer was quoted in the report as saying: "How much mud do I have to sift through in that population to find that diamond?

"A reasonable amount... we've got a finite resource in terms of people hours and finite budget in terms of cost to target there."

Working-class accents were disliked by managers who conducted job interviews, the report found, and many were impressed by young people who had travelled

widely – a luxury which often favours those from well-off families.

Labour leadership contender, Andy Burnham, is today expected to address Britain's "flawed" education system, and will blame the "vast majority" of MP's private education for a lack of focus on alternative university routes.

In a speech today Mr Burnham is expected to say that university-style student funding should be extended to young people who decide to study for technical qualifications.

The study by Royal Holloway, University of London, on behalf of the Commission, was based on interviews with staff from 13 elite accountancy, law and financial services firms.

The report found that elite firms are "systematically excluding bright working-class applicants" from their workforce.

To break into top jobs, state school candidates needed higher qualifications than privately educated peers, it added.

Between 40% and 50% of job applications to the study's firms were made by applicants who had attended Russell Group universities.

These applicants received 60% to 70% of all job offers.

Candidates from fee-paying and selective schools made up 70% of graduate trainees at case study firms.

Some people took to social media to highlight that, in the long term, employers would be missing out on some great talent.

15 June 2015

⇨ The above information is reprinted with kind permission from The Huffington Post UK. Please visit www.huffingtonpost.co.uk for further information.

© 2015 AOL (UK) Limited

Has social mobility collapsed?

By Patrick Worrall

The claims

"In every single sphere of British influence, the upper echelons of power in 2013 are held overwhelmingly by the privately educated or the affluent middle class.

"New Labour promised social improvement but delivered a collapse in social mobility."

Sir John Major, 13 November 2013

The background

Sir John Major delivered a broadside against class-ridden modern Britain this week, bemoaning the over-representation of the privately educated among the nation's high achievers.

The former Tory Prime Minister, who went to a grammar school in south London, told Conservative activists: "To me, from my background, I find that truly shocking. I remember enough of my past to be outraged on behalf of the people abandoned when social mobility is lost."

The speech was interpreted in some quarters as a veiled attack on the former public schoolboys who dominated Eton-educated David Cameron's cabinet, although Sir John was careful to blame New Labour for what he called a "collapse in social mobility".

Today Mr Cameron responded, saying: "I absolutely agree with the thrust of what John Major said. You only have to look at the make-up of Parliament, the judiciary, the Army, the media. It's not as diverse, there's not as much social mobility as there needs to be."

Has there really been a collapse in social mobility? And is the rest of Britain as dominated by independent school alumni as the Coalition front bench?

The analysis

Private schools

Last year the Sutton Trust, a think tank that specialises in social mobility, found that 68 per cent of "public servants" (including royalty and people who work in national, public or local government organisations) went to private schools.

Some 63 per cent of leading lawyers were privately educated, as were 60 per cent of the upper ranks of the armed forces. Independent schools produce more than half of the nation's leading journalists, diplomats, financiers and business people.

Only 6.5 per cent of all British children and 18 per cent of pupils over 16 go to private schools, so there is an apparent concentration of power in the hands of a minority in many influential sections of society.

The Sutton Trust's figures are not historical, so we generally can't say whether the situation has got better or worse in recent years.

Parliament is an exception. While there are fewer private school alumni in the Commons now than there were in the 1970s and 1980s, the percentage has gone up in the last three parliaments.

Social mobility

Measuring social mobility involves a lot more than finding out where people went to school.

Academics make a distinction between absolute social mobility – the total number of people changing their class or status – and relative

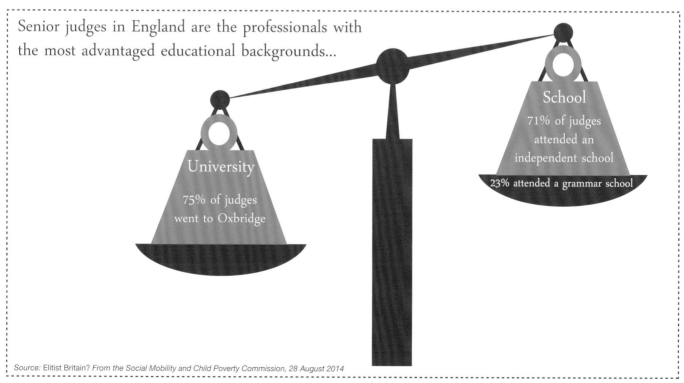

Senior judges in England are the professionals with the most advantaged educational backgrounds...

University
75% of judges went to Oxbridge

School
71% of judges attended an independent school
23% attended a grammar school

Source: Elitist Britain? *From the Social Mobility and Child Poverty Commission, 28 August 2014*

social mobility, which refers to your chances of moving up the ladder compared to someone else from a different class (how likely is your low-born FactChecker to better himself, compared to the rich boy in the next postal district?).

Sir John is not alone in assuming that social mobility has gone backwards in recent years. This appears to be a widespread belief, much of it traceable to research carried out by the London School of Economics (LSE) for the Sutton Trust in the mid-2000s which found that the earnings of children born in 1970 were more similar to the income of their parents than children born in 1958.

Dr John Goldthorpe from Oxford University says these findings helped shape a "consensus view" about social mobility among politicians and commentators on the left and right.

The received wisdom is that there was a golden age of upward mobility for working-class children after World War Two. The trend was perhaps linked to grammar schools – and the theory comes with an unbeatable selection of poster boys in the form of grammar school alumni like Paul McCartney, Michael Caine and Richard Burton. Everyone agrees that it has now ground to a halt.

Dr Goldthorpe thinks this is nonsense. He says the influential LSE study was flawed, and the best evidence shows "no decline in mobility, absolute or relative, occurred in the late 20th-century".

The only notable change was that upward mobility among men, which increased for most of the twentieth century, began to level off towards the end of it, partly because men were facing more competition from women entering the labour market.

A number of different studies chime with this view. A Cabinet Office report for Tony Blair found that intergenerational class mobility was high for most of the 20th century but the picture did not change much.

There was no post-war golden age followed by a slump. Britain did not become a more open or fluid society.

Should we bring back grammar schools?

If Dr Goldthorpe is right, the high rates of absolute social mobility last century had little to do with education and more to do with changes to the economy that created more "room at the top": an expansion of professional and managerial jobs that needed to be filled.

The introduction of grammar schools appears to have made no difference overall to the chances of working-class children climbing the ladder, according to this 2011 paper, because "any assistance to low-origin children provided by grammar schools is cancelled out by the hindrance suffered by those who attended secondary moderns".

Earlier this month the Institute for Fiscal Studies, in another Sutton Trust-funded paper, found that pupils eligible for free school meals or who live in poorer neighbourhoods are significantly less likely to go to a grammar school.

We don't know whether that was true in the 1960s, but if Dr Goldthorpe is right, it is a fair assumption that richer families will always use their resources to out-compete others when it comes to securing a better education for their children.

He writes: "Parental – and, perhaps, grandparental – resources, even if not sufficient to allow for children to be educated in the private sector, are still widely deployed to buy houses in areas served by high-performing state schools, to pay for individual tutoring, to help manage student debt, to support entry into postgraduate courses for which no loans are available, or, in the case of educational failure, to fund 'second chances'."

International comparisons

A 2010 study of developed countries in the OECD group found that Britain had the worst intergenerational income mobility of all the countries studied.

One suggested explanation for this is a link between income inequality and poor social mobility.

US economists pioneered the use of the beautifully named 'Great Gatsby curve' to measure this.

The UK scores badly for both inequality and social mobility in most Great Gatsby curves.

The verdict

Sir John Major is quite right to say that the privately educated still dominate the upper echelons of British life, if the Sutton Trust's numbers are correct.

And there is less opportunity to climb the ladder of opportunity in the UK than in many other developed countries.

But the evidence for a recent "collapse in social mobility" is weak.

It could be argued that no such collapse took place. One persuasive, if depressing, theory is that people's chances of transcending their class origins remained about the same over the whole of the last century.

If that theory is true, the implication is that bringing back grammar schools would not help to accelerate social mobility, and the Government would do better to concentrate on income inequality rather than education policy.

14 November 2013

⇨ The above information is reprinted with kind permission from Channel 4. Please visit blogs.channel4.com for further information.

© Channel Four Television Corporation 2015

Cameron's 'one nation' mission to improve life chances for all

The PM will set out his plan for extending opportunity in Britain, with stronger families, improved education and a welfare system that helps people into work.

In a key note speech, the Prime Minister will say there was a persistent failure by previous governments to deal with stalled social mobility and a lack of economic opportunity for many people.

Mr Cameron will say that dealing with this issue and improving people's life chances will be central to his approach to the next five years in government and a key aim of his 'one nation' ideal.

The Prime Minister, David Cameron, will say:

"Today I want to make a bigger, and deeper, argument about how we realise the 'one nation' ideal and help everyone achieve their full potential. When it comes to extending opportunity – there is a right track and a wrong track.

"The right track is to recognise the causes of stalled social mobility and a lack of economic opportunity. Family breakdown. Debt. Addiction. Poor schools. Lack of skills. Unemployment. People capable of work, written off to a lifetime on benefits.

"Recognise those causes, and the solutions follow. Strong families that give children the best start in life. A great education system that helps everyone get on. A welfare system that encourages work – well paid work.

"These are the drivers of opportunity – and we need to extend them. The wrong track though, is to ignore the causes, and simply treat the symptoms of the social and economic problems we face.

"Take for example the complacency in how we approach the crucial issue of low pay. There is what I would call a merry-go-round. People working on the minimum wage having that money taxed by the Government and then the Government giving them that money back – and more – in welfare.

"Again, it's dealing with the symptoms of the problem – topping up low pay rather than extending the drivers of opportunity – helping to create well paid jobs in the first place.

"So this is the change we need. We need to move from a low wage, high tax, high welfare society to a higher wage, lower tax, lower welfare society.

"I am proud that in the past five years, we have begun to turn the tide on the failed approach. We've put strengthening families, reforming education and transforming welfare at the heart of what we have been doing. But in the next five years we have to go so much further – and that begins by recognising something really fundamental.

"So many of our country's efforts to extend opportunity have been undermined by a tolerance of government failure. The failure to look after children in care. The tolerance of sink schools that have failed one generation after another. An acceptance of long-term unemployment among hard-to-reach individuals.

"We have to end the complacency that has sometimes infected our national life, that says some problems are too big, and we can put up with second best. For me, when it comes to extending opportunity, the next five years will be about a complete intolerance of this government failure."

The Prime Minister will set out three key strands of work:

Stronger families

The Government will continue to bring forward action to support parents with more childcare, flexible working and relationship support, alongside more action to speed up the adoption process and expand the Troubled Families programme to help 400,000 families over the next five years.

First-class education

There will be a zero tolerance of failing schools with legislative action and a new focus on 'coasting schools' – those regarded as requiring improvement – that will require standards to be turned round or the school to be turned into an academy.

Well-paid jobs

From October 2015, the value of the minimum wage will go up to £6.70. And the Government will increase personal tax threshold to £12,500 over the next five years. As the economy recovers the Government will go further, while continuing to take action on welfare to ensure work is always a better option to a life on benefits.

22 June 2015

⇨ The above information is reprinted with kind permission from the Prime Minister's Office, 10 Downing Street and The Rt Hon. David Cameron MP. Please visit www.gov.uk for further information.

© Crown copyright 2015

Do grammar schools boost social mobility?

***An article from* The Conversation.**

By Matt Dickson, Prize Fellow in the Department of Social and Policy Sciences, University of Bath, Lindsey Macmillan, Senior Lecturer in Economics, UCL Institute of Education and Simon Burgess, Professor of Economics, University of Bristol

THE CONVERSATION

The role grammar schools should play in English education is still hotly contested, more so today than it has been in years. This is despite the fact that there are only 164 grammar schools operating in England today (out of more than 3,000 state secondary schools), a huge decline from their sixties heyday.

Part of the reason for the heat in the debate is the proposal from some on the right of British politics that grammar schools should be fully revived as a way to boost social mobility. Our recent research on the grammar school system re-ignited this debate, with both pro- and anti-grammar commentators claiming support from it for their position.

"A select few individuals from poorer backgrounds do benefit from the grammar system, but the vast majority will not go to a grammar school, and are therefore more likely to end up lower down the earnings distribution"

But by leaving aside the obvious questions – whether access to grammar schools is fair (no) and what grammar schools can do for marginal students (open to debate) – we can avoid the more overheated parts of the debate, and instead address a trickier problem: the implications selective school systems might have for longer-term earnings inequality.

"Selective schooling systems have consequences for those who don't get in as well as those who do"

Like with like

We did this by using a nationally representative data source, Understanding Society 2009–2012. For our study, we considered the adult earnings distribution for over 2,500 individuals born between 1961 and 1983, comparing those who grew up in selective-school areas with those who grew up in comprehensive-schooling systems.

We matched comprehensive-schooling areas to selective-school areas based on average hourly wage, unemployment rate, and the proportion of private schools in each area. The data also allowed us to control for parental education and occupation when an individual was 14, gender, age, ethnicity and current area of residence.

After introducing these controls, we were able to compare the adult earnings of people who look very similar – except that some grew up in an area operating a selective system and others in one with a comprehensive system.

The spread

When we considered these two groups, we saw that average earnings in each group were very similar: almost exactly £8.60 per hour. Earnings inequality however was greater for those who grew up in areas operating a selective system compared to those who grew up in comprehensive areas.

One way to compare the degree of inequality in each distribution is to look at the standard deviation, which captures how widely spread earnings are around their

average level. Comparing individuals with similar characteristics, the standard deviation of earnings for those who grew up in selective areas was £5.41 per hour – substantially higher than the £4.81 deviation in non-selective areas.

"The role grammar schools should play in English education is still hotly contested, more so today than it has been in years"

Another way to quantify the inequality is to look at the difference in pay between those at the 90th percentile of the wage distribution and those at the 10th percentile. For those who grew up in a selective system, this figure is £13.14 an hour, whereas it's £10.93 an hour for the comprehensive system.

This means that those who grew up in the selective system and go on to be top earners take home £24,000 more per year than those at the bottom of the distribution, whereas for people growing up in the comprehensive system the corresponding difference is just under £20,000.

"It seems clear that grammar systems increase inequality, lowering earnings at the bottom as well as raising them at the top. So why do some still champion them as a surefire way to boost social mobility?"

Those comparisons look at the difference between the top and the bottom of each distribution, but we can also compare the top of the selective system distribution and the top of the comprehensive distribution. What we found was that those who grew up in a selective system and ended up earning at the 90th percentile earned £1.31 an hour more (statistically significant) than comparable individuals who grew up in a comprehensive system. At the other end of the scale, if you grow up in a selective system and don't do so well, earning at the 10th percentile, you earn 90p an hour less than the similar individual who also grew up in a comprehensive system – a statistically significant gap.

Those at the top do relatively better in the grammar system, while those at the bottom do worse. These differences are statistically significant. We can also see that it is not until the 70th percentile that the selective earnings distribution climbs above the non-selective one.

Still dreaming

It seems clear that grammar systems increase inequality, lowering earnings at the bottom as well as raising them at the top. So why do some still champion them as a surefire way to boost social mobility?

The reason is well illustrated by Toby Young's glib response to our research. Social mobility arguments for grammar schools focus exclusively on the impact they have on the top of the earnings distribution for the 25–30% of children who make it into one. The impact there is indeed positive, and our research does show that: those at the top who come from the grammar system do earn more.

The argument then runs that grammar schools promote social mobility by enabling bright kids from poorer backgrounds to access these schools and go on to achieve high earnings and status.

"Those at the top do relatively better in the grammar system, while those at the bottom do worse"

But what we have shown is that there is another side to this story – what the selective system does to those at the bottom of the distribution. At that end, individuals who do not make it to the grammar school do worse than they would have done if they had grown up in an area with a comprehensive school system.

We might also refer to the evidence that selective systems sort children more by where they are from than by ability – and soon, it becomes clear that selective systems are not the social mobility boosters that their champions claim them to be.

A select few individuals from poorer backgrounds do benefit from the grammar system, but the vast majority will not go to a grammar school, and are therefore more likely to end up lower down the earnings distribution than if they grew up in an area operating a comprehensive system.

The debate about grammar schools will no doubt continue to rage – but what we cannot ignore is that selective schooling systems have consequences for those who don't get in as well as those who do.

18 June 2014

⇨ The above information is reprinted with kind permission from *The Conversation*. Please visit www.theconversation.com for further information.

© 2010-2015, The Conversation Trust (UK)

Public attitudes towards social mobility and in-work poverty

Social mobility today

⇨ 65 per cent of the public thought 'who you know' matters more than 'what you know'.

⇨ Three in four people said family background has significant influence on life chances in Britain today.

⇨ However, when asked about the extent to which their own parents' income or level of education had influenced where they had got to in life, people were less clear. Four in ten thought that their parents' income and education had influenced them and four in ten thought it had not.

⇨ 29 per cent of those who thought family background influences life chances thought it was more important now than in the past, 36 per cent thought it was less important and 37 per cent thought its influence had remained the same.

⇨ Seven in ten people thought a good education was the key to getting a good job. But nearly half thought it remained out of reach for most children from lower-income families.

⇨ Public opinion on the influence of education on future employment prospects varied by country; fewer people in Scotland (63 per cent) and Wales (59 per cent) thought a good education was the key to getting a good job than in England (72 per cent).

⇨ When asked where government should be focusing its efforts to improve social mobility, the most commonly selected policies related to employment. Six in ten said the most important way for government to improve social mobility was by either creating jobs or apprenticeships or helping unemployed young people to find work.

In-work poverty

When given statistics on the percentage of children in poverty whose parents are in work:

⇨ Two in three thought government had a role in tackling in-work poverty.

⇨ Three in four thought that government should top-up incomes of those in in-work poverty.

Even more people thought employers had an important role to play:

⇨ More than four in five (84 per cent) said that employers should be providing more opportunities for progression for their employees.

⇨ More than four in five (84 per cent) said that employers should be paying wages that better reflect the cost of living.

Attitudes on factors that influence social mobility and trends over time

Most people think that personal connections are an important influence on life chances in Britain today

Respondents were asked: to what extent do you agree or disagree that, in Britain today, 'who you know' matters more than 'what you know'?

⇨ Overall, 65 per cent agreed that 'who you know' matters more than 'what you know'. 17 per cent disagreed.

⇨ There was little variation between different population groups. However, there was a very high level of agreement among people with apprenticeship level qualifications (83 per cent).

The majority of people think family background has a significant influence on life chances in Britain today

Respondents were asked: to what extent do you agree or disagree that, in Britain today, family background significantly influences an individual's chances of doing well in life?

⇨ Overall, 76 per cent agreed and 11 per cent disagreed family background significantly influences an individual's chances of doing well in life.

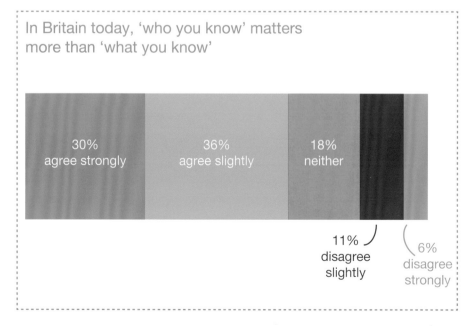

In Britain today, 'who you know' matters more than 'what you know'

- 30% agree strongly
- 36% agree slightly
- 18% neither
- 11% disagree slightly
- 6% disagree strongly

- ⇨ Agreement that family background influences life chances increased with age and income. Graduates were most likely to agree (83 per cent).

- ⇨ The most advantaged socio-economic groups were more likely to agree.

- ⇨ Ethnic minority groups were less likely to agree (70 per cent).

- ⇨ Disagreement was higher among students (15 per cent) and people not in work (15 per cent).

People were less likely to think that their own success (or otherwise) was a result of their family background

Respondents were asked: to what extent do you agree or disagree that your parents' income when you were growing up has influenced where you have got to in life?

- ⇨ Overall, 41 per cent agreed and 41 per cent disagreed their parents' income had influenced where they had got to in life.

- ⇨ Agreement was higher among students (53 per cent), parents (46 per cent) and ethnic minority groups (58 per cent).

- ⇨ Agreement was lower amongst older people. Just 35 per cent of the 55+ age group agreed.

Respondents were also asked: to what extent do you agree or disagree that your parents' level of education has influenced where you have got to in life?

- ⇨ Overall, 43 per cent agreed and 42 per cent disagreed their parents' level of education had influenced where they had got to in life.

- ⇨ Agreement was higher among parents (49 per cent), ethnic minority groups (58 per cent) and graduates (51 per cent).

- ⇨ Disagreement was higher amongst the older (55+) group (47 per cent).

There was disagreement about whether family background was becoming more or less important to life chances than in the past (or staying the same)

Respondents were asked: is family background more or less important in influencing where people end up in life than it was in the past?

- ⇨ Overall, 35 per cent felt that family background was becoming less important than it was in the past; 29 per cent felt that it was becoming more important; and 35 per cent felt that it was the same as before.

- ⇨ People who were unemployed and those from less advantaged social groups (DE) were more likely to think family background was becoming more important (37 per cent).

- ⇨ People from ethnic minority groups were less likely to think the importance of family background was declining (27%).

The majority of people think education is key to chances of getting a good job; but nearly half do not believe that a good education is accessible to all

Respondents were asked: to what extent do you agree or disagree with the following statement?

... a good education is the key to getting a good job

- ⇨ Overall, 72 per cent agreed that a good education is the key to getting a good job; 18 per cent disagreed.

- ⇨ Agreement increased with salary (those earning over £26k) (83 per cent) and among graduates (78 per cent).

- ⇨ Agreement was higher amongst the most advantaged groups.

- ⇨ Agreement was lowest among under 35s (65 per cent) and in Scotland (63 per cent) and in Wales (59 per cent).

... a good education remains out of reach for most children from lower income families

- ⇨ Overall, 49 per cent agreed that a good education is out of reach for most children from lower income families; 38 per cent disagreed.

- ⇨ Agreement was highest among ethnic minority groups (65%). Agreement was also higher among people from lower socio-economic groups, people not in work (56 per cent), with no qualifications (57 per cent), on lower incomes (51 per cent) and among men (51 per cent vs 46 per cent of women).

Education was seen as the most important factor influencing chances of getting a top job

- ⇨ Education/qualifications were the most commonly cited factor seen to be important to chances of getting a top job; (72 per cent) followed by self-confidence/self-belief (61 per cent).

- ⇨ When respondents were asked to state which was the single most important factor, more people cited education/qualifications than any other response (34 per cent).

June 2013

- ⇨ The above information is reprinted with kind permission from the Social Mobility and Child Poverty Commission. Please visit www.gov.uk for further information.

© Crown copyright 2015

Time for professions to follow the best examples and judge ability to do the job not "holidays you've been on, places you've visited"

The Social Mobility Foundation echoes the call by the Social Mobility and Child Poverty Commission to make access to a top job genuinely meritocratic and suggests they follow the examples of the leading firms in their fields.

Research published by the Commission shows that too many firms are judging candidates on factors 'associated with middle class-status' as their definition of talent. Such a definition will almost always exclude the young people the Social Mobility Foundation works with, who are mostly eligible for free school meals, get the right grades to enter such professions but do not have the same access to resources to be formed in the same image of those interviewing them.

Commenting on the report, the Chief Executive of the Social Mobility Foundation, David Johnston said:

"It is often said by the representatives of our elite professions that they 'don't care where people come from, they just want the best people' which is a catchy phrase but shown by this report not to be true.

"Those firms that have privately looked at the performance of their employees based on their entry requirements have found no correlation with factors such as past academic performance or university attended and their best performers.

"But as today's report makes plain, there is still a pervasive attitude in some of our professions that all the best people can be found in a very small segment of the country's population and even that, in the words of one of those quoted in the report 'homogeneity breeds a huge amount of efficiency in organisations'. Such an attitude lies at the heart of why these professions are so unrepresentative of the country at large.

"Many firms such as J.P. Morgan, Linklaters, KPMG, Clifford Chance and CH2M work with the SMF on a range of initiatives to find the brightest and best whatever background they come from and many have hired young people they've worked with as a result.

"It is time that firms committed to the actions that others have been taking: opening work experience opportunities, paying internships, creating effective non-graduate routes, widening the range of universities they target and making sure that in their recruitment practices they're judging potential to do the job, not someone's background and the patronising notion they 'couldn't be put in front of a client'."

1. The Social Mobility Foundation is a charity that helps young people from low-income backgrounds enter universities and top professions. www. socialmobility.org.uk.

2. The core programme the SMF runs, the Aspiring Professionals Programme, features a mentor from your chosen profession, university application support (trips to universities, workshops on applying to university, aptitude tests and interviews), work placements and skills sessions across the sixth-form and university years.

3. Interviews with young people currently in sixth-form, at university or employed in the professions can be arranged as well as with representatives at firms that have been taking action by calling 0207 183 1189.

15 June 2015

⇨ The above information is reprinted with kind permission from the Social Mobility Foundation. Please visit www.socialmobility.org.uk for further information.

I see your school performance was tops. What a pity it wasn't the right school!

© Social Mobility Foundation 2015

Further education and social mobility

So what's going on? Record levels of employment, dramatic falls in unemployment, and yet no real rise yet in felt levels of wealth and well-being? Does a lack of social mobility explain any of this? And if it does what is the role of FE in providing any of the solutions?

By Nick Isles

First to the productivity conundrum. At the time of writing, the latest jobs numbers showed that the UK unemployment rate fell to 6.2% over the three months to the end of July, its lowest level since 2008. And yet average weekly earnings still lagged way behind inflation. And so did productivity.

The latest estimates show productivity collapsing since 2009. If there isn't additional productivity it means that there is less likely to be additional profits. More productivity should translate into higher margins per hour worked or unit of capital invested. The answer to this conundrum is that the UK has entrenched itself into a low-productivity economic cycle where cheap labour has substituted for investment in new technologies. This enables more growth and lower levels of unemployment which are unequivocally good things but does not allow for much wage growth since profits are spread more thinly.

However, since the publication of Thomas Picketty's book, (*Capitalism in the 21st Century*) earlier this year many people have been alerted to the fact that the wealthy top 1% – or even top 0.1% – have been accumulating a greater and greater share of capitalism's profits to themselves over the last 30 years. This means we now have income distribution charts that resemble those that might have been drawn in 1918. The closing of income inequality has gone sharply into reverse.

Worse still, returns to accumulated wealth now outstrip the potential to gain wealth through income for this group. This means the ladder has been drawn up for all but the select or lucky few. The Resolution Foundation has shown that those who run companies or 'own the means of production' have been taking 12–14% more of the profits created than was the case 30 years ago. With less profit going to the many and more to the top few there is less spending available to the whole economy since those with more tend to save more than those with less. This has some unfortunate consequences the results of which we have just lived through in the Great Recession of 2008–2012.

Often this wealth accumulation has gone hand-in-hand with a narrowing of the establishment or elite. To illustrate this point, in the UK the Government's Social Mobility and Child Poverty Commission showed that 71% of senior judges, 62% of senior armed forces officers, 55% of top civil servants and 43% of newspaper columnists went to a select group of private schools and Oxbridge. This is a quite staggering level of un-diversity.

What is also unique about the type of inequality that is happening now is that it is those in the middle of the income distribution who have stood still for longer. Their earnings have not increased in real terms for over a decade in the UK and longer in the US. Much of the

panoply of social policies designed to narrow income distribution are simple anti-poverty policies of one form or another. This includes child benefit payments; working tax credits; additional services for the poor families, etc. The success here is that in aggregate rising employment levels have stopped excessive rises in poverty (though rises there have been since 2008).

The widening of the gap between the middle and the very top is driven by some deep-seated trends such as investment available for education; so-called assertive mating where people marry people like themselves; and geographical segregation to name but three. Of these education is perhaps the most important and the area where policy can have the biggest impact. And this is where FE comes in.

Given the role education plays in driving social mobility, spending less on education would seem to be a madness. But this is what we have done over the last five years compared with the previous 50 years. The Institute for Fiscal Studies calculate that real cuts to education spending amount to around 3.5% in real terms during the life of this parliament. So one obvious answer is to spend more on education and invest more in your local FE college in particular. The reason for this is that FE colleges cater to an enormously wide and diverse population. If we really want to kick-start the engine of social mobility we need to invest in those institutions that the people we need to be more socially mobile attend. But how to do this? My colleague Julie Mills in her recent blog http://www.mkcollege.ac.uk/listing/julie-mills-blog/detail/social-mobility-costs-money-and-it%E2%80%99s-time-to-start-spending-it argued for a hypothecated education tax or a guaranteed share of the local business rates. Another idea would be to hypothecate a wealth tax to education spending. Apart from more cash in the round, investment in the professionals who deliver the education would also not go amiss.

Of course much of the social mobility debate goes to the very heart of the sort of capitalism we want to develop. Neo-liberalism has birthed a return to 19th-century levels of inequality and elites drawn from ever narrower backgrounds. This surely cannot be the right vision for the 21st-century good society.

18 September 2014

⇨ The above information is reprinted with kind permission from FE News and Gavin Isles. Please visit www.fenews.co.uk for further information.

© FE News/Gavin Isles 2015

Digital divide in the UK

What's the challenge?

In a digital world, computer skills are becoming more and more important. How can we make sure the most vulnerable sectors of UK society aren't excluded and the Internet is accessible to everyone?

The importance of digital equality

Today, computer skills and knowledge of the Internet can connect people to new and better jobs, open up the opportunity of flexible working from home, cheaper forms of communication and social interaction to community infrastructures and government services, improve access to learning opportunities and provide access to more convenient and often cheaper products and online services.

Digital inequality matters because those without access and the right combination of access, skills, motivation and knowledge are missing out on important areas of the digital world. This doesn't just impact on individual lives but on families, communities, political processes, democracy, public services and the economic and social health of the nation as a whole.

Research shows a clear correlation between digital exclusion and social exclusion. This means that those already at a disadvantage and arguably with the most to gain from the Internet are the least likely to be making use of it and become further disadvantaged by not using it.

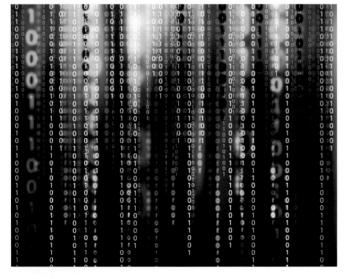

What are the barriers to getting online?

1. Access

Affordability of equipment or usage. Even though prices for ICT equipment and connection time will almost certainly continue to decrease, cost will still remain a significant barrier for some excluded groups, even in the long term.

Facts

- 5.9 million adults in the UK have never used the Internet
- There are 4.1 million adults living in social housing that are offline
- The South East had the highest proportion of recent Internet users (90%) and Northern Ireland was the area with the lowest proportion (80%)
- 27% of disabled adults (3.3 million) had never used the Internet
- Adults aged 16 to 24 years have consistently shown the highest rates of Internet use
- Between 75% and 90% of jobs require at least some computer use
- Offline households are missing out on estimated savings of £560 per year from shopping and paying bills online. Source: ONS 2015, National Housing Federation, The Tinder Foundation

Pricing structures, as well as price itself, has an effect on take-up. For instance, the rapid adoption of mobile phones even by low-income groups is probably largely a result of more flexible and non-excluding pricing structures (such as 'pay-as-you-go' packages) than of traditional fixed-line telephone services. Internet take-up among low-income groups has been much lower. Research has shown that non-users of the Internet estimate the cost of use to be far higher than it actually is.

Lack of time to take training courses, or to travel to an Internet café or UK online centre – or prioritising other activities over learning how to make use of technologies.

Lack of training or support in learning how to use a personal computer or the Internet.

Low literacy levels – People are sometimes more willing to admit to a lack of knowledge about computers than to illiteracy. On the other hand, evaluation of UK online centres has found that engaging with computers and the Internet has enabled people to identify and discuss literacy and numeracy difficulties which they had never addressed before.

Disabilities which may make accessibility devices or improvements in design necessary in order to make effective use of technologies.

Poor usability of interfaces – such as relevant websites – may also be an issue preventing effective use.

2. Motivation

Lack of interest or perceived need – Large numbers of people report that the reason they do not use the Internet is that they have no need for it, or no interest. These numbers have fallen as the numbers of people using the Internet have increased. But, as of February 2006, the ONS still found that 39% of non-internet users (representing 13% of the total adult population) said that they do not want to, need to, or have an interest in using the Internet.

Cost/benefit ratio too high – Even if some benefit or interest in using the Internet is assumed, it may be judged that the benefit is too small to justify what may be a high-value investment in computer equipment. Again, more affordable pricing schemes and flexible technologies may change this.

Lack of appropriate content – Provision of stimulating and/ or useful content is crucial in attracting new users to ICT. The bias of existing content towards the social, cultural and economic priorities of earlier-adopters may act as a considerable disincentive to people trying to engage in new technologies.

3. Skills and confidence

Skills – Use of all ICT, and particularly of a traditional personal computer, is not straightforward, and may not be intuitive. The Skills for Life survey in 2003 found that large proportions of the population were not able to complete a series of basic functions using a Windows-based computer – even among regular computer users. In the consultations conducted as part of the Inclusion Through Innovation study, more respondents cited lack of training or skills as a problem which may prevent some groups from benefiting from ICT than those who cited lack of access. Touch-screen and more intuitive design is helping improve this.

Confidence in ability – Particularly a problem among those who do not have immediate family or friends who are internet users, and so do not get the help and guidance which many new users find valuable.

Concerns about security or undesirable material being available on the Internet. This may affect both take-up and willingness. The Oxford Internet Survey in 2005 found that, among existing users, majorities are concerned about viruses (82% of computer users), unpleasant experiences when using email (60% of email users), and putting their privacy at risk (54% of internet users). Non-users have also been reported to have similar (though less specific) concerns – although also often recognising that these are factors to be aware of, rather than insurmountable barriers to internet use.

⇨ The above information is reprinted with kind permission from the Royal Geographical Society (with IBG). Please visit www.21stcenturychallenges. org for further information.

© Royal Geographical Society 2015

The myth about social mobility in Britain: it's not that bad, says new report

THE CONVERSATION

An article from **The Conversation.**

By Stephen Gorard, Professor of Education and Public Policy, Durham University

It is generally accepted by all political parties and most of the media that social mobility in the UK is low compared to other countries, and worsening over time. These 'facts' appeared in the manifestos of all three major parties at the last election. This has led to the creation of a mobility tsar and the expenditure of billions of pounds of public funding.

So how is it possible that the Organisation for Economic Co-operation and Development (OECD), in a report out today, reports very high upward inter-generational educational mobility in the UK and a very strong link between education and subsequent earnings?

Education at a Glance suggests that more of the adult population of the UK, aged 25 to 64, is educated to higher education (university graduate) level than in any other EU country. This rose from 25.68% of adults in 2000 to 40.98% in 2012. And the earnings difference between having an upper secondary qualification and a degree (or equivalent) is high: a person with a degree in the UK will earn 55% more.

Education appears to matter. In every generation, a sizeable proportion achieve a qualification higher than that of their parents. But as the qualification level of the population grows, the proportion 'outperforming' their parents decreases – and would eventually cease if everyone achieved a university-level qualification.

The UK also has one of the lowest links in the EU between an individual's background (as assessed by economic, social and cultural status) and attainment in the OECD's 2012 Programme for International Student Assessment (PISA). This measure of equity is better than in Denmark, for example, and almost twice as good as in Hungary and France.

Resolving the apparent contradiction

The OECD figures have a mixture of survey sources, and do not always present response rates and the reasons for missing country data. So there will be some inaccuracy in their figures, which they acknowledge. But a much more likely reason for these two vastly different accounts is that the research report on which so many politicians and other commentators have based their views of social mobility makes some crucial mistakes.

The report that started all of the trouble was published in 2005 by the Sutton Trust. It used the 1958 and 1970 GB birth cohort studies to suggest that inter-generational income mobility for those born in 1970 was worse than for those born in 1958.

And it also claimed that mobility was worse in Britain than in similarly developed countries like Norway. It justifed this claim by comparing the data for Norway in 1958 with that for Britain in 1970. No satisfactory explanation has ever been given for this. If you use instead the 1958 data for Britain – which makes sense not only because it is closer in time to Norway's 1958 data, but also because the parental income measures are more similar – social mobility is about the same as in Norway and all other comparator countries.

The same data looked at sensibly seems to show considerable income mobility between generations. Around 17% of those born to the poorest 25% of families in Britain go on to become among the richest 25% in one generation. As the new OECD study suggests, some of this may be due to the high educational mobility of the UK.

> **"It is generally accepted by all political parties and most of the media that social mobility in the UK is low compared to other countries"**

The opportunity cost

Considerable effort and funding is therefore being put into a solution to a problem that does not appear to exist – perhaps because good news in not so popular as bad. But there is a real opportunity cost. Real problems for the most educationally disadvantaged in the UK, such as adults without prior qualifications and low levels of literacy, are being ignored.

Hopefully this new OECD picture will provide some commentators with the courage to look again at social mobility, and begin to distinguish between those elements of our education that should be treasured and those that need urgent attention.

9 September 2014

⇨ The above information is reprinted with kind permission from *The Conversation*. Please visit www.theconversation.com for further information.

© 2010-2015, The Conversation Trust (UK)

Worse than Rwanda: life prospects in Britain's poorest areas

The 18-year gap in active lifespan between richest and poorest in modern Britain.

By John Bingham, Social Affairs Editor

Babies born in the poorest parts of the UK today have worse prospects for a long and healthy life than those born in Rwanda, official figures show.

New estimates of 'Healthy Life Expectancy' – the length of time people would normally expect to lead a full and active life in good health – show a gap of more than 18 years between the richest and poorest parts of England.

The figures from the Office for National Statistics also call into the question the assumption that members of the baby boom generation will enjoy a long and carefree retirement, with half of men and 40 per cent of women likely already to be in poor health before they reach pension age.

Based on current health trends and death rates, it is estimated that a baby boy living in a neighbourhood classed as being within the most deprived ten per cent of England is likely to live 74.1 years but only 52.2 years in generally 'good' health.

By contrast a boy born the same day in one of the least deprived ten per cent of areas would have 83.1 years to live on average and 74 years in good health.

Girls born in the most deprived areas of England are expected to live 52.4 years in 'good' health, compared with 71.3 years for those in the richest areas.

The gap of more than 18 years in male Healthy Life Expectancy (HLE) at birth mirrors the contrast between the developed and developing worlds.

According to figures from the World Health Organization, average male HLE in Rwanda currently stands at 55 years, almost three years longer than in the poorest parts of England.

The estimate for boys in the most deprived parts of England is on a par with those for Botswana, Gambia, Guyana and Djibouti and only two years more than that for those born in Burkina Faso, one of the poorest countries in the world.

Duncan Exley, director of the Equality Trust think-tank, said: "The UK is one of the most unequal countries in the developed world.

"This is damaging our health, our social bonds and our economy – 82 per cent of Brits think inequality has gone too far.

"Unless the Government adopts a clear target to reduce inequality, it will have to deal with a country and an economy that are unnecessarily unhealthy."

Janet Morrison, chief executive of Independent Age, the charity working with older people, said: "The huge difference in how long people can expect to live in good health demonstrates why it is meaningless to talk about a generation of wealthy, carefree pensioners.

"The reality is that many older people will be approaching retirement age having already experienced many years of poor health and will have relatively few years ahead of them.

"It demonstrates why it is essential that we focus efforts on measures to help prevent older people from becoming ill in the first place and on having excellent health and social care services for them if they do."

5 March 2015

⇨ The above information is reprinted with kind permission from *The Telegraph*. Please visit www.telegraph.co.uk for further information.

© Telegraph Media Group Limited 2015

New research exposes the 'glass floor' in British society

Less able, better-off kids are 35% more likely to become high earners than bright poor kids.

New research, conducted by Abigail McKnight of the London School of Economics for the Social Mobility and Child Poverty Commission, has exposed the reality of a 'glass floor' in British society that protects less able, better-off children from falling down the social ladder as they become adults.

Alan Milburn, Chair of the Social Mobility and Child Poverty Commission, said that the 'glass floor' is as much a problem as the 'glass ceiling' in inhibiting social mobility in Britain.

The research uses the British birth cohort survey to look at the impact that social background has on earnings at age 42 and whether this can be explained by early cognitive ability, qualifications, school type, parental education level and non-cognitive skills such as self-esteem and behaviour.

It finds that children from more advantaged social backgrounds who are assessed at age five as having low cognitive ability are nonetheless significantly more likely to become high earners than their high-ability peers in lower-income households. Children from high-income backgrounds who show signs of low academic ability at age five are 35% more likely to be high earners as adults than children from poorer families who show early signs of high ability.

The research finds that social background and family income have a significant effect on the likelihood of being a high earner even after controlling for meritocratic factors such as cognitive and non-cognitive ability and qualifications achieved. Parental education level and attendance at a private school or a grammar school all have a significant independent impact over-and-above their impact on academic attainment. Remarkably, the research also finds a clear correlation between the social background of a child's grandfather and eventual labour market success.

The research concludes that better-off, middle-class parents are successful in effectively creating a 'glass floor' which protects their children from downward mobility and makes it harder for able children from less advantaged backgrounds to succeed.

The research suggests there are two main pillars supporting the 'glass floor':

1. More advantaged parents securing educational opportunities to help their children overcome lack of ability and overtake their more gifted but poorer peers by:

   - investing time and resources in education to help children showing early signs of low attainment to recover and achieve good qualifications and even to enter higher education – a major stepping stone to a professional job

   - providing better careers advice and guidance – this is likely to be important in explaining why parental education has such a big impact on their children's earnings even controlling for qualifications and schooling

   - placing a high value on polish and 'soft skills', such as self-confidence, decisiveness, leadership and resilience

   - prioritising school choice, with more advantaged parents able to move house to be in the catchment area of a great state school, invest in private tuition to coach their children to pass the 11+ in selective areas, or give their children a private education.

2. More advantaged parents securing advantages for their children into the labour market that are unavailable to less well-off parents by:

   - helping their children into employment through informal social networks

   - securing informal and unpaid internships

   - investing in their children's 'soft skills' which are highly valued in employment recruitment processes.

Chair of the commission, Alan Milburn said:

"No one should criticise parents for doing their best for their children. That's what we all want. But

What is the 'glass ceiling'?

The 'glass ceiling' is an invisible and unacknowledged barrier that prevents a person progressing in their career. It is especially relevant for women, minorities and those from disadvantaged backgrounds.

What is the 'glass floor'?

A recent report from the Social Mobility & Child Poverty Commission suggests that well-off parents create a 'glass floor' that prevents their children from 'falling down the social ladder' even if they are less able.

Britain is a long way from being a meritocratic society when the less able can do better in life than the more able.

"It has long been recognised that there is a glass ceiling in British society that prevents children with potential progressing to the top. This research reveals there is a glass floor that inhibits social mobility as much as the glass ceiling.

"It's a social scandal that all too often demography is still destiny in Britain. The Government should make its core mission the levelling of the playing field so that every child in the country has an equal opportunity to go as far as their abilities can take them.

"A one-nation approach means giving disadvantaged kids access to the support, advice and development opportunities that better-off middle-class families take for granted.

"Employers also need to step up to the plate by ensuring that internships aren't simply reserved for those with the right social contacts and that recruitment processes aren't skewed to favour polish over potential."

London School of Economics Senior Research Fellow Dr Abigail McKnight said:

"The fact that middle-class families are successful in hoarding the best opportunities in the education system and in the labour market is a real barrier to the upward social mobility of less advantaged children."

"Children from less advantaged families who show high potential at age five are struggling to convert this potential into later labour market success.

"Schools could do much more to help children from less advantaged families build on high early potential."

The research makes several key policy implications including:

⇨ educate parents to improve their skills and perspectives: reducing inequalities in parental education through adult skills programmes, given there appears to be a direct link between parental education and child outcomes

⇨ ensure children from less advantaged backgrounds have access to the support and opportunities available to their peers: providing opportunities for them to build non-cognitive and 'soft skills', providing good careers information and guidance, mentoring and a rich set of opportunities to understand the world of work

THE GREAT SOCIAL SUCCESS RACE
READY, SET, GO!

⇨ tackle material deprivation and the financial pressures on parents that undermine their efforts to give their kids the best possible start in life

⇨ tackle the institutional barriers to aspiration: improving school quality in disadvantaged areas, improving access to high-quality schools and universities (e.g. admissions procedures), and removing financial barriers to higher education

⇨ take action to reduce 'opportunity hoarding': including tackling unpaid internships, encouraging employers to remove barriers in the recruitment process that inadvertently prevent those with high potential from disadvantaged backgrounds being successful, and ensuring school selection procedures don't inadvertently skew access towards those from advantaged backgrounds who can afford extensive private tuition.

26 July 2015

⇨ The above information is reprinted with kind permission from the Social Mobility and Child Poverty Commission. Please visit www.gov.uk for further information.

© Crown copyright 2015

Should students from state schools be given priority access to university?

***An article from* The Conversation.**

By Vikki Boliver, Senior Lecturer in Sociology and Social Policy, School of Applied Social Sciences, Durham University and Stephen Gorard, Professor of Education and Public Policy, Durham University

THE CONVERSATION

Higher education is seen by some as a passport to social mobility, a leveller which can help young people from disadvantaged backgrounds catch up with their more fortunate peers by offering them a springboard from which to enter the world of employment.

But repeated studies have told us that students from poorer families, boys and some ethnic groups are less likely to participate in higher education than other groups – and even less likely to attend the most prestigious institutions.

One way of widening participation in higher education is through the use of contextual admissions policies. This involves taking into account the socioeconomic context of students' academic achievements when deciding which university applicants to shortlist, interview, make standard or reduced offers to, or accept at confirmation or clearing.

The idea behind the use of contextual data in university admissions is, as the 2004 Schwartz report on fair admissions put it, that: "it is fair and appropriate to consider contextual factors as well as formal educational achievement, given the variation in learners' opportunities and circumstances".

Some have argued that type of school attended should be a factor in university admissions decisions and have called for state school students to be admitted with lower grades than their privately educated peers. But how appropriate is the type of school a student attended as a contextual factor?

State school students do better at university

Research on degree outcomes published recently by the Higher Education Funding Council for England (HEFCE) found that state school students do better, on average, at degree level than their privately educated peers.

In 2013–14, 82% of state school graduates achieved a first or upper second-class degree compared to 73% of graduates from private schools. This nine percentage point gap was found to decline to four percentage points after differences in grades on entry to university were taken into account. The gap was narrower for those with very high grades on entry, at about one percentage point for those who enter with AAAA at A-level.

The Higher Education Funding Council for England (HEFCE) reported very similar findings last year and some 12 years ago. Studies carried out at the universities of Bristol, St Andrew's and Oxford reported similar results, although a Cambridge study found no link between school type and degree performance.

> **"Some have argued that type of school attended should be a factor in university admissions decisions and have called for state school students to be admitted with lower grades than their privately educated peers"**

What causes this difference? It is often said that state schools are less well-resourced – at least compared to the well-known private schools. As a result, the reasoning goes, able students at state schools are less likely to achieve grades that do full justice to their ability while private schools are better placed to help even lower-ability students achieve high grades. However, the truth is that we do not know.

Either way, the gap in degree performance between students from different types of school has been used as evidence to support the case for contextualised admissions as a means of making university access fairer and widening participation. But would it be fairer to base contextualised admissions policies on school type – and would it help to widen participation?

It depends on the school

It is questionable whether attending a state school rather than a private school counts as being contextually disadvantaged for all state school students. The differences are only 'on average'. Many state schools serve students from highly privileged backgrounds whose family resources are similar to their privately educated peers – and these schools often achieve results as good as or better than many private schools. It would probably be these relatively advantaged state school students who would benefit first and foremost from a

contextualised admissions policy based on school type. Far more so than state school students from working-class families and comparatively deprived communities.

The HEFCE study also compared students from neighbourhoods with higher education participation rates in the bottom and top 20% nationally and found that those from the bottom 20% are about three percentage points less likely to receive a first or upper second class degree on average after taking into account grades on entry. Similarly, HEFCE's study published last year and other research found coming from a more deprived neighbourhood to be associated with poorer performance at degree level.

"It is questionable whether attending a state school rather than a private school counts as being contextually disadvantaged"

All of this suggests that it may not be the most socioeconomically disadvantaged section of the state school population that is driving the slightly superior average performance of state school pupils at degree level, but rather the socioeconomically advantaged section of the state school population.

What does this mean?

A lot of the above needs further research and analysis. But our current conclusion would be that coming from a state school, by itself, is not a good enough reason to say a student is likely to have more potential to succeed in higher education and so should be prioritised for access to university. We are much more likely to correctly identify students from disadvantaged contexts if we consider indicators of their individual circumstances and neighbourhood characteristics as well.

It also becomes clear that success in higher education should not be the justification for bringing in a policy of contextualised admissions. This is because socioeconomically disadvantaged students may underachieve relative to their potential in higher education as well as earlier in their school careers, precisely because they continue to be socioeconomically disadvantaged.

Therefore, applicants should not be given priority merely because they are from state schools – this would not solve anything and there must be better ways to ensure that access to universities is fair for everyone.

22 September 2015

⇨ The above information is reprinted with kind permission from *The Conversation*. Please visit www.theconversation.com for further information.

© 2010-2015, The Conversation Trust (UK)

24% of MPs went to Oxbridge, compared to less than one in 100 of the public.

Amongst MPs:

- 33% went to Independent schools
- 25% went to Grammar schools
- 40% went to Comprehensive schools

Key facts

⇨ The Great British Class Survey of 161,000 people, has charted the emergence of a new class system comprising seven groups in Britain, blurring the conventional boundaries between the 'middle' and 'working' classes. (page 1)

⇨ According to GBCS, only 39 per cent of Britons now fit the stereotypes of middle and working class. (page 1)

⇨ Seven new class groups have been identified:

  • Elite

  • Established middle class

  • Technical middle class

  • New affluent workers

  • Traditional working class

  • Emergent service workers

  • Precariat (the precarious proletariat) (page 2)

⇨ Children from low-income families are less likely to be judged 'above average' at reading, despite having similar scores to their comparison counterparts on the reading test. Pupils from higher income families had a 52.3 per cent chance of being rated as 'above average' in reading, compared to 26.6 per cent for low-income pupils. (page 6)

⇨ Children who speak other languages in addition to English are less likely to be judged 'above average' at reading than children only speaking English – despite scoring the same in the tests. (page 6)

⇨ Black African and Bangladeshi pupils score relatively highly on the reading test – but are again less likely to be judged 'above average' and more likely to be judged 'below average' by their teacher. (page 6)

⇨ Three of the highest offices in Britain are held by men who attended Eton and Oxbridge. The Mayor of London went to Eton and Oxford, the Prime Minister went to Eton and Oxford, the Archbishop of Canterbury went to Eton and Cambridge. (page 10)

⇨ A new study conducted in collaboration with Facebook using anonymised data from the social networking site shows a correlation between people's social and financial status, and the levels of internationalism in their friendship networks – with those from higher social classes around the world having fewer friends outside of their own country. (page 11)

⇨ Switzerland, the USA and Belgium are the top-three countries in the world when it comes to net per capita financial assets. (page 12)

⇨ Between 2010 and 2012, life expectancy for women born in Dorset (relatively affluent) was 86.6 years, compared with 78.5 years in Glasgow (relatively deprived); men aged 65 in Harrow (relatively affluent) could expect to live for another 20.9 years versus 14.9 years in Glasgow (ONS, 2014). (page 15)

⇨ The majority of British adults (56%) say senior professions are unfairly dominated by people from affluent middle-class backgrounds. 31% say they are open to people of all backgrounds. (page 18)

⇨ Only 6.5 per cent of all British children and 18 per cent of pupils over 16 go to private schools. (page 23)

⇨ 65 per cent of the public think 'who you know' matters more than 'what you know'. (page 28)

⇨ Two in three think the Government has a role in tackling in-work poverty. (page 28)

⇨ Three in four think the Government should top-up incomes of those in in-work poverty. (page 28)

⇨ Overall, 35 per cent feel that family background is becoming less important than it was in the past; 29 per cent feel that it was becoming more important; and 35 per cent feel that it was the same as before. (page 29)

⇨ Research published by the Commission shows that too many firms are judging candidates on factors 'associated with middle class-status' as their definition of talent. (page 30)

⇨ Based on current health trends and death rates, it is estimated that a baby boy living in a neighbourhood classed as being within the most deprived ten per cent of England is likely to live 74.1 years but only 52.2 years in generally 'good' health. (page 35)

⇨ Children from more advantaged social backgrounds who are assessed at age five as having low cognitive ability are nonetheless significantly more likely to become high earners than their high-ability peers in lower-income households. (36)

⇨ Repeated studies have told us that students from poorer families, boys and some ethnic groups are less likely to participate in higher education than other groups – and even less likely to attend the most prestigious institutions. (page 38)

Blue-collar worker

This refers to someone who is in a traditionally working-class job – that is, manual labourers (based on the idea that historically, manual and industrial workers would wear overalls to work which were often blue).

Elite

This is the most privileged group in the UK. They are set apart from the other six classes, especially because of their wealth, and they have the highest levels of all three capitals.

Emergent service workers

This new, young, urban group is relatively poor but has high social and cultural capital.

Established middle class

This is the second wealthiest class group and it scores highly on all three capitals. It is the largest and highly gregarious class group and scores second highest for cultural capital.

Middle England/Middle Britain

Middle England (or sometimes, Middle Britain) is increasingly used as a socio-economic reference point instead of middle class. It encompasses a wider range of characteristics than simply income, career and education, although there is no single definition. It can be seen as overlapping with other social groups identified by politicians, such as Ed Miliband's 'squeezed middle' and Nick Clegg's 'Alarm Clock Britons'.

New affluent workers

This young class group is socially and culturally active, with middling levels of economic capital.

Precariat (the precarious proletariat)

This is the poorest, most deprived class and scores low for social and cultural capital.

Social class

Class refers to a hierarchy which exists among social groups in the UK. Traditionally, people belonged to one of three classes – working, middle and upper – based on the status ascribed to them by their occupation and economic position. Massive social and economic shifts in the 20th century led to what many felt was the death of social class, but most would argue that a class system still exists in a different form and is a major part of the collective British consciousness today. It has become a very complex (not to say contentious) issue to define one's social class, factoring in such issues as background and upbringing, accent, manners, culture, education, career and postcode as well as wealth.

Social engineering

Attempting to fix social problems and manufacture a social system to a pre-decided pattern.

Social mobility

The ability of an individual to move around within the class system. In the past, social mobility was an almost unheard-of concept, whereas today we would think little of the daughter of a builder growing up to become an accountant, or a doctor's son forgoing higher education and training as a plumber. However, there are worries that the progress of social mobility in the UK is slowing.

Technical middle class

This is a small, distinctive new class group that is prosperous but scores low for social and cultural capital. It is distinguished by its social isolation and cultural apathy.

Traditional working class

This class scores low on all forms of capital, but is not completely deprived. Its members have a reasonably high house values, which is explained by this group having the oldest average age (66 years).

Underclass

This is a term which is used to describe a group who they feel ought not to be described as working class, since they do not work. It refers to those who exist within what is often called the 'dependency culture': a social group who do not earn but instead subsist on state benefits. Like 'chav', the term has been accused of creating a negative stereotype of working-class people and demonising those who require state welfare.

White-collar worker

This refers to someone who is in a traditionally middle-class career – a professional, or clerical worker (based on the idea that historically, male office workers would wear a white dress shirt to work).

Assignments

Brainstorming

⇨ In small groups, discuss what you know about social mobility and social class. Consider the following points:

- What is social mobility?

- What is social class?

- What are the traditional social classes identified in British society?

- How does education affect social mobility?

Research

⇨ The article on page 11 suggests that people from higher social classes have fewer international friends. Conduct a survey amongst your year group to find out how many international friends your peers have.

⇨ Choose a well-known person that you like or admire (this could be a politician, musician or film star). Research their education and background. Make some notes and then, as a class, discuss your findings. How many of your chosen celebrities come from privileged backgrounds?

Design

⇨ Design a poster that illustrates the seven new social classes identified in the article on page one. You should create cartoons to demonstrate each of the classes.

⇨ Choose one of the articles in this book and create an illustration to highlight the key themes/message of your chosen article.

⇨ Design a leaflet that illustrates the findings from the article Public attitudes towards social mobility and in-work poverty on page 28.

⇨ In small groups, create a poster that displays typical conceptions/stereotypes of each social class (upper, middle and working).

Oral

⇨ As a class, discuss whether you believe that young people from disadvantaged backgrounds should be given priority access to University places.

⇨ In pairs, debate whether you think Grammar schools are a positive or negative concept.

⇨ "Employers should focus purely on the grades you have achieved at school or University, not extra-curricular activities or gap years!" Debate this statement as a class.

⇨ What would you say defines a person's class? Is it only about income, or are there other factors involved? Do you think people still tend to identify themselves as belonging to a particular class in today's society? Discuss with a partner.

Reading/writing

⇨ Write a one paragraph definition of social mobility.

⇨ Write a one paragraph definition of social class.

⇨ Read Social class in 21st-century Britain: where is the divide now? on page three. The author uses the examples of Made in Chelsea and The Only Way is Essex to demonstrate the increasing similarities between social classes. Go through the article and, in two columns, list the similarities and differences highlighted between the classes.

⇨ What reasons do the British Sociological Association give for why middle-class people are more likely to play music, paint and act? Make some notes and compare with a classmate.

⇨ Write a blog post that explores how education affects social mobility.

⇨ Read Digital divide in the UK on page 32 and write an article for your school newspaper exploring the importance of digital access for social mobility.

⇨ Watch an episode of the ITV period drama Downton Abbey. How have society's attitudes to social class evolved since the period in which the drama was set? Are there any ways in which the class distinctions shown in the programme have not changed?

⇨ Write three diary entries, covering a typical day in the life of a working-class person in 1915, 1955 and 2015. What employment would they be likely to have? What would their prospects be? How would their daily lives differ, and in what ways would there be similarities?

HAVERING COLLEGE OF F & H E

193831

Acknowledgements

The publisher is grateful for permission to reproduce the material in this book. While every care has been taken to trace and acknowledge copyright, the publisher tenders its apology for any accidental infringement or where copyright has proved untraceable. The publisher would be pleased to come to a suitable arrangement in any such case with the rightful owner.

Images

All images courtesy of iStock.

Icons on pages 27 and 38 courtesy of AllSilhouettes. com. Icons on page 41 courtesy of Freepik.

Illustrations

Don Hatcher: pages 10 & 30. Simon Kneebone: pages 4 & 26. Angelo Madrid: pages 20 & 37.

Additional acknowledgements

Editorial on behalf of Independence Educational Publishers by Cara Acred.

With thanks to the Independence team: Mary Chapman, Sandra Dennis, Christina Hughes, Jackie Staines and Jan Sunderland.

Cara Acred

Cambridge

January 2016